# SHAKESPEARE AND THE DANCE

# SHAKESPEARE AND THE DANCE

Alan Brissenden

HUMANITIES PRESS

Atlantic Highlands, New Jersey

© Alan Brissenden 1981

*First Published in the United States of America 1981 by*
HUMANITIES PRESS INC.
*171 First Avenue, Atlantic Highlands, New Jersey 07716.*

*Printed in Hong Kong*

---

**Library of Congress Cataloging in Publication Data**

---

Brissenden, Alan.
    Shakespeare and the dance.

    Includes bibliographical references and index.
    1. Shakespeare, William, 1564–1616—Knowledge—
Performing arts.   2. Dance in literature.   I. Title.
PR3034.B7  1980              822.3'3              80–12067
ISBN  0–391–01810–8

---

*To the memory of my father,*
*who first showed me Shakespeare,*
*and my mother, who taught me to dance*

# Contents

# List of Plates

# Preface

For help of various kinds in the preparation of this book I owe debts of gratitude to several institutions and many individuals. Encouragement to work on Shakespeare's use of dance came first through an invitation from B. A. W. Jackson to speak at the 1968 Shakespeare Seminars at Stratford, Ontario, and subsequently I had the pleasure and good fortune to give papers on the subject at the 14th Congress of the Australasian Universities Language and Literature Association, in Dunedin; the Shakespeare Institute, Birmingham, at the invitation of Terence Spencer, whose untimely death robbed the world of a great Shakespearian and a good man; at the Humanities Research Centre, Canberra, by invitation of the Director, Ian Donaldson; and at Monash University, through the request of Philip Ayres. The Australian Broadcasting Commission invited me to write a long radio feature on dance and the Elizabethans and the handsome fee for this helped to further my investigations.

Much of the research was done during two periods of study leave granted by the University of Adelaide, during the second of which I was also assisted by an emergency grant from the University's Research and Publications Fund and a travel grant from the British Council, awarded under its excellent Commonwealth Universities Interchange Scheme.

Parts of the book have appeared in some form in the following, and I am grateful to the respective publishers for permission to draw on this material: *Shakespeare and the New World*, Stratford Papers 1968–9, ed. B. A. W. Jackson (McMaster University Library Press and Irish University Press, Shannon, 1972); *Shakespeare and Some Others*, ed. Alan Brissenden (Adelaide University, Adelaide, 1976); *Cahiers Elisabéthains* (Montpellier) 13, 1978; *Review of English Studies*, n.s. xxx, 117 (1979).

The staffs of libraries in which I have worked have invariably been courteous and co-operative, particularly those of the British Library, the Bodleian and, most frequently used, the Barr Smith

Library of the University of Adelaide. Time was saved and information found for me by Irene Cassidy in London, Julia Rowbotham and Margaret Davies in Oxford, and Robin Eaden in Adelaide.

A large number of people have gladly shared their learning and good sense with me – practically, in conversations and by letter. For comments on the manuscript at different stages I am particularly grateful to my brother Bob and to my friends and colleagues Tim Mares, John Colmer and Kevin Magarey. The office staff of the Adelaide University English Department has kept its patience, collectively and individually, through various typings of the chapters.

Mabel Dolmetsch's *Dances of England and France 1450–1600* (London, 1949) introduced me to many of the dances known to Shakespeare and led me to the original sources, especially Thoinot Arbeau's *Ochésographie* (Lengres, 1589), a copy of which was in Thomas Bodley's library in the early seventeenth century. Belinda Quirey, by her teaching, turned bare words into movement for me.

As always the greatest debt is to my wife, for her invaluable criticism and for helping me so delightfully to understand why dancing is love's proper exercise.

*Adelaide*                                                        A.B.
*1979*

# 1 Dance and the Elizabethans

> Learne then to daunce you that are Princes borne
> And lawfull Lords of earthly creatures all;
> Imitate them, and thereof take no scorne,
> (For thys new Art to them is naturall)
> And imitate the starres cælestiall.
>    For when pale Death your vitall twist shall sever,
>    Your better parts must daunce with them for ever.
>                  Sir John Davies, *Orchestra*

The achievement of order in a fractured world is a major theme in all of Shakespeare's plays. He began writing for the theatre just as the Elizabethan age reached its peak of magnificence, with the defeat of the Spanish Armada, and during his lifetime, as the period of greatness waned, questions of hierarchy in government and society were brought increasingly into open debate. Queen Elizabeth could tell the historian William Lambarde, 'I am Richard II; know ye not that?'[1] in acknowledgement of the insecurity of her throne, even though it was tacitly agreed that she held it by divine right. Her less subtle successor aggressively proclaimed his belief in divine monarchy, in *Basilikon Doron*, the book he wrote for his elder son, Prince Henry, for example, and in such public statements as his speech to Parliament on 21 March 1610:

> The state of Monarchy is the supremest thing upon earth; for kings are not only God's lieutenants upon earth and sit upon God's throne, but even by God himself they are called gods.[2]

Four years later James's court spawned the scandal of the Overbury murder, as malevolent as anything in Webster or Middleton, an example of corruption in high places which could have served for the 'cursed example' of Antonio's first speech in *The Duchess of Malfi*:

> A prince's court
> Is like a common fountain, whence should flow
> Pure silver-drops in general. But if 't chance
> Some cursed example poison't near the head,
> Death and diseases through the whole land spread.
>
> (I. i. 11–15)

Disorder in the state resulting from discord in the affairs of those in authority is the basic action of many of Shakespeare's plays, but even the tragedies, which deal with the extremes of human suffering, present a view of life which is optimistic at the most fundamental level, the view that order is possible, that harmony can be restored. Closely related to this attitude is his use of dance both as part of the visually presented stage picture and as the content of dialogue. In some plays, *Romeo and Juliet*, *A Midsummer Night's Dream* and *The Winter's Tale* among them, dance is essential to the dramatic action; in many, particularly the history plays, it provides material for imagery; *Much Ado About Nothing* and *Twelfth Night* are but two in which references to dance illuminate character. An understanding of dance and of particular dances themselves adds much to an appreciation of many of the plays and it is indispensable for the proper comprehension of certain scenes and passages.

An awareness of dance during the period also adds to our understanding of both the Elizabethan theatre and the society of the time; further, it can help our perception of the relationship between the two. Although it had long been under attack by the church, dancing had a firm and vital place in English life, particularly in the country, where the seasonal round of the year was marked by festivals. Many of these had dances characteristic of specific times and places, like the hobby-horse and floral dances of May Day in the West country, the more ubiquitous maypole itself, and the morris dances of Whitsuntide. Alongside these ritual dances, rehearsed and mostly performed by the few, were the popular dances which were part of celebration at any time or place – longways dances, with no top, bottom or leader, for instance, rounds in which the ring of dancers broke and reformed, changed and reassembled, or chain dances, with running steps and simple interlacing figures. During the sixteenth century and first half of the seventeenth, dancing became ever more important at the English court. Country dances were taken up, and formal dancing developed in variety and complexity, reaching its most extravagant presentation in those symbolic theatrical expressions of monarchic power, the Stuart masques.[3] In the theatre, dancing from both court and country became part of the living fabric of drama.

From classical times onward the dance had been a symbol of harmony and concord, and in the elaborate entertainments of the Renaissance courts especially this symbolism was supported by spectacle of costume and setting. The cosmic dance, the rhythmic movement of all things in relation to one another, lasted until the eighteenth century beside the great chain of being and music itself as a commonly accepted metaphor of order, a concept closely allied to the Pythagorean belief in the primacy of number, that pervasive philosophy which affected so many corners of Renaissance thought and activity.[4] Translating a snatch of Boethius, for example, the Elizabethan mathematician John Dee wrote,

All thinges (which from the very first originall beeing of thinges haue beene framed and made) do appeare to be Formed by the reason of Numbers. For this was the principall example or patterne in the minde of the Creator.[5]

Since number and pattern are essential to it, dance was seen as the means by which order came out of primal chaos. Plato mentions the idea in his *Laws* (653e) and the *Timaeus* (47e), and the satirist Lucian deals with it in detail in his dialogue on dancing. Even though Lucian is being ironic, his use of these ideas indicates their general acceptance when he was writing in the second century. His dialogue provided a major source for theories of the creation of the world by means of the dance of atoms, and the dependence of the universe for its equilibrium on the joyous dance of the heavenly bodies.

In Sir John Davies' nimble expression of these notions in his poem *Orchestra* (1594) Prince Antinous tries to persuade Penelope to dance by saying, .

> *Dauncing* (bright Lady) then began to be,
> When the first seedes whereof the world did spring,
> The Fire, Ayre, Earth and Water did agree,
> By Loves perswasion, Natures mighty King,
> To leave their first disordred combating;

And in a daunce such measure to observe,
As all the world their motion should preserve.

Twenty-five years later, Robert Burton wrote in his compendious
ragbag of Renaissance thought, *The Anatomy of Melancholy* (1621):

> The Sun and Moon (some say) dance about the earth, the three
> upper Planets about the Sun as their centre, now stationary, now
> direct, now retrograde, now in apogee then in perigee, now swift,
> then slow, occidental, oriental, they turn round, jump and trace,
> Venus and Mercury about the Sun with those thirty-three
> Maculae or Bourbonian planets, dancers about the harping Sun,
> saith Fromundus. Four Medicean stars dance about Jupiter, two
> Austrian about Saturn &c., and all (belike) to the musick of the
> Spheres.[6]

Another divine, Jehan Tabourot, who cloaked his religious identity
under the anagram 'Thoinot Arbeau', ended his dance manual
*Orchesography* (1589) by saying to his pupil: 'Practise these dances
carefully and you will become a fit companion of the planets, which
dance of their own nature . . . '.[7]

Davies' poem draws to a close with a glorious vision of the 'bright
moon' surrounded by 'a thousand sparkling stars' which 'moved in
such measure/To do their sovereign honour and delight' – a 'divine
image [of] our glorious English court'. Queen Elizabeth was
frequently presented in literature and art in this central position;
King James's wife, tall, plain Anne, arranged to embody the
symbol, giving it life in court masques in which she appeared. For
Jonson's *Masque of Queens* (1609), for instance, she became
Bel-Anna, Queen of the Ocean. Similarly, Prince Henry
appeared as the fairy prince himself in the marvellous *Oberon* (1610)
and, much later, Charles I and Henrietta Maria impersonated such
emblematic characters as Philogenes, the Lover of his People, and
the Chief Heroine, sent down from Heaven by Pallas, in Davenant's
*Salmacida Spolia*, the last of these inward-looking celebrations of
royal authority. This final spectacle was prepared and presented by
the king and queen during the unpropitious days of January 1640.

Although Queen Elizabeth did not appear in masques as the
Stuart royal ladies delighted to, she was, like her father, a notable
dancer, and in 1589 John Stanhope, gentleman of the Privy
Chamber, wrote to Lord Talbot, 'My Lord, the Queen is so well as I

assure you, six or seven galliards in a morning, besides music and singing, is her ordinary exercise'[8] – a galliard would have been a far more spiritually and aesthetically satisfying form of exercise than many of today's mechanical movements. Nearly ten years later the French Ambassador, André de Maisse, remarked that 'without doubt she is a mistress of the art, having learnt in the Italian manner to dance high'.[9] This may have referred to the volta,[10] a lively dance which was a favourite of the Queen, in which the lady is lifted into the air by her partner, and the steps include high leaps and turns. In her old age the Queen danced less, but enjoyed watching others, rebuking her maids if they did not keep time. On 28 April 1602, in her sixty-eighth year, she opened a ball at Richmond with the Duke of Nevers; if the dance really was a galliard, as has been reported, it is unlikely that the queen, sprightly as she was even then, took the liveliest part.[11] It is more probable that she formally began the evening by leading the French Duke in a stately processional pavan, which was usually followed by a galliard. Arbeau gives the following graceful description of such occasions:

On solemn feast days the pavan is employed by kings, princes and great noblemen to display themselves in their fine mantles and ceremonial robes. They are accompanied by queens, princesses and great ladies, the long trains of their dresses loosened and sweeping behind them, sometimes borne by damsels. And it is the said pavans, played by hautboys and sackbuts, that announce the grand ball and are arranged to last until the dancers have circled the hall two or three times, unless they prefer to dance it by advancing and retreating. Pavans are also used in masquerades to herald the entrance of the gods and goddesses in their triumphal chariots or emperors and kings in full majesty.[12]

The galliard gave men particularly the chance to show their grace and agility, with leaps, turns in the air, rapid kicks and intricate footwork.

In a court led by Queen Elizabeth, dancing was an essential accomplishment for both ladies and gentlemen. According to one of his few enemies, Sir Christopher Hatton 'came into court "by the galliard", for he came thither as a private gentleman of the Inns of Court in a masque; and for his activity and person, which was tall and proportionable, taken into [the Queen's] favour'.[13] He eventually leaped high enough to become her Lord Chancellor. The entertainment in which Hatton first caught the Queen's attention was probably the masque given at Whitehall after the performance of *Gorboduc* on 18 January 1562 by the Gentlemen of the Inner Temple, a repeat performance of part of the Christmas festivities of the Inner Temple in 1561 in which Hatton was Master of the Game and Robert Dudley, later to be the Earl of Leicester, was Governor of the festival and the Christmas Prince, Pallaphilos.[14]

The Inns of Court were not simply the law schools of the time; they were considered to be a third university and the place to acquire gentlemanly skills. Dancing was a recreation and an exercise to give final polish and as regular ceremonial it formed part of the established corporate life of the Inns from before 1471 until at least 1733.[15] It is a significant coincidence that the most complete dance instructions in English known before the publication of John Playford's *Dancing Master* in 1651 (the preface of which mentions the 'sweet and ayry Activity' of the gentlemen of the Inns of Court) are to be found in six manuscripts, all among the papers of men who had been Inns of Court students. Three are in the Bodleian Library, including the earliest, a commonplace book of about 1570 which has fifteen dances (MS Rawl. Poet. 108, ff. 10–11); instructions for seven and the name of one other were written out by the astrologer and antiquarian Elias Ashmole, probably in the 1630s (MS Rawl. d. 864, fo. 199); and the most interesting, the commonplace book of John Ramsay, has twenty-one (MS Douce 280). The British Library has a manuscript with eight dances (MS Harl. 367, ff. 178–9), the library of the Middle Temple one with ten (Misc. vol. XXVII) and the Royal College of Music another with eight (MS 1119). What is remarkable is that even though at least fifty years, and probably more, lie between the writing of the earliest and the latest of these important sources for dance history, they all have the names of six dances in common, copied down in the same order. Variations in the instructions for the dances indicate that the steps were modified over the years; but even though they were not precisely identical throughout all the time, the manner of their listing shows not only a continuing tradition of dancing at the inns, but, more interestingly, a continuing tradition of the same dances, and of ritualised performance. The six shared by all the manuscripts are the Quadran Pavan, Turkeyloney, the Earl of Essex Measure, Tinternell, the Old Almain and the Queen's Almain. The Black Almain is common to five of the manuscripts, and the Cicillia Almain is found in four. These are all court dances, not the rounds, hays and hornpipes of the country, but several in these lists must have been known outside the Inns of Court, since the tunes for the Cicillia Pavan, the Nine Muses and the New Almain are suggested as melodies for ballads printed in *A Handefull of pleasant delites*, a small anthology of 1584.

John Ramsay describes his twenty-one dances under the heading 'Practise for Dauncinge'. Conveniently, he also includes in his commonplace book an autobiography which relates that he was born in 1578, was admitted to Peterhouse in Cambridge in 1601, then withdrew from the university and joined the court. He became absolutely weary of that 'tedious life'[16] and, on inheriting wealth at his father's death, entered the Middle Temple on 23 March 1606. He travelled on the Continent and in the Holy Land between 1613 and 1616, settled down to married life in 1620 then went on a voyage to Guiana in 1623, as the last, shakily written, entry tells us. The dances he records can be safely dated between 1606 and 1613.

Bulstrode Whitelocke, who was Master of the Revels at the Middle Temple in 1628, has left a detailed description, written about eight years later, of ceremonial on All Saints Day, and while critical of the way in which the students' dancing has deteriorated to 'bare walkinge'[17] he says that the leading gentleman is asked by the Judges to sing, and while dancing (or walking!) he begins a psalm which all the gentlemen, presumably following him, then take up. These were 'Solemn Revels', which began with the measures, slow and stately, similar to if not exactly the same as the pavan. Faster dances followed as the Post Revels – galliards, corantos, brawls, almains and country dances. Interestingly, this was exactly the pattern of the final dances of the court masque: when the chief masquers came down from the stage to take out the guests on to the floor of the hall, they first danced the measures and then followed these with the more lively, energetic dances. Whether there is a connection between the structure of the Solemn Revels and Post Revels at the Inns of Court and the final dances of the court masques has yet to be explored. What is certain is that many courtiers were at one time Inns of Court men.

The learning and practice of dancing at the Inns is consistent with the training of a gentleman as laid down by several influential writers including Richard Mulcaster, whose pupils from the Merchant Taylors' school performed masques and interludes before Queen Elizabeth; Roger Ascham, who advises learning to 'daunce cumlie' among his list of 'pastimes that be fitte for Courtlie

Gentlemen'; and the great arbiter of behaviour, Baldassare Castiglione, who, despite his nationality, was much admired by Ascham, a noted Italophobe. In his much translated and reprinted *Book of the Courtier*, Castiglione encourages his reader to 'daunce well without ouer nimble footinges or to busie trickes' in public, keeping such ostentatious 'swiftnesse of feete and doubled footinges' to the privacy of his own chamber.[18] Castiglione is among those who advise against dancing too energetically in public because the sweat produced may offend the rest of the company.

The longest discussion of dancing printed during the sixteenth century in England is in *The Book named the Governor* (1531) by Sir Thomas Elyot, who was 'not of that opinion that all dancing generally is repugnant unto virtue' although he realised that dancing 'of the more part of sad [i.e. serious] men is so little esteemed'.[19] After an engaging description of the Platonic idea of the dance of the heavenly bodies, Elyot goes on to moralise the dance, first as symbolising concord between a man and a woman and then as a means of teaching the moral virtue of prudence. He demonstrates this by matching the five figures of the basse dance with different ingredients of prudence. The honour, a bow for the man and a curtsy for the woman, reminds us that 'at the beginning of all our acts, we should do honour to God'. The brawl, or branle, which seems to have been a rocking, stationary step, he sees as signifying 'maturity – a mean between two extremities, wherein nothing lacketh or exceedeth', a nice introduction of Aristotelian thought. The singles, in which one foot glides forward and is then joined by the other, are 'two unities, separate in passing forward; by whom may be signified providence and industry'. The reprise, in which the feet move back, so that the dancer retreats, 'may well be called circumspection' and the doubles, in which one foot moves forward and pauses while the other glides up to it, then pauses while the first moves on, is for Elyot 'compact of the number three, whereby it may be noted these three branches of prudence: election, experience, and modesty. By them the said virtue of prudence is made complete, and is in her perfection.'

Early in his discussion, which is in effect an apology for dancing, Elyot suggests that dance is a good recreation 'to recomfort and quicken the vital spirits' lest they become overtired with mental effort; he ends by saying that it is 'as well a necessary study as a noble and virtuous pastime'. He gives one chapter each to hunting and archery, and to other exercise three chapters, but he devotes seven to dancing, an indication of his enthusiasm for the art and the need to defend it. The basse dance, which he uses as his exemplar, is hardly the jolliest of measures, though he may have chosen it because it was well-known, even if already going out of fashion in courtly circles. *The Governor* was published just ten years after the first dancing instructions in English were printed; these were *The maner of dauncynge of bace daūces after the vse of Fraunce*, translated by Robert Coplande and appended to a little book on how to write and speak French.[20] This had appeared in 1521, and may indicate Coplande's acumen in cashing in on the popularity of things French at Henry VIII's court in the year after the Field of the Cloth of Gold rather than the popularity of the basse dance itself, which does not appear in any of the manuscript sources noted earlier and was certainly out of fashion in France by the time of Arbeau, who says it has been replaced by the pavan. The two dances share similar steps, which result in a gliding, undulating movement, and it would appear that the later dance, the origins of which are obscure, developed from the earlier. As well as being used specifically, 'basse' is a generic term for 'low' dances, in which the feet remain close to the ground, in contrast to 'haut' dances like the volta and the galliard, with their springings, leaps and turns.

The basse dance is not even among those listed humorously by Barnaby Rich in the 'Epistle Dedicatorie' to his *Farewell to Military Profession* (1581):

> As firste for Dauncyng, although I like the Measures verie well, yet I could neuer treade them a right, nor to vse measure in any thyng that I went aboute, although I desired to performe all thynges by line and by leauell, what so euer I tooke in hande.

> Oure Galliardes are so curious, that thei are not for my daunsyng, for thei are so full of trickes and tournes, that he whiche hath no more but the plaine Sinquepace, is no better accoumpted of then a verie bongler, and for my part, thei might assone teache me to make a Capricornus, as a Capre in the right kinde that it should bee.

> For a Ieigge my heeles are too heauie: And these braules are so busie, that I loue not to beate my braines about them.

> A Rounde is too giddie a daunce for my diet, for let the dauncers runne about with as muche speede as thei maie: yet are

thei neuer a whit the nier to the ende of their course, vnlesse with
often tourning thei hap to catch a fall. And so thei ende the
daunce with shame, that was begonne but in sporte.

These Hornepipes I haue hated from my verie youth: and I
knowe there are many other that loues them as euill as I.

Thus you maie perceiue that there is no daunce but either I
like not of theim, or thei like not of me, so that I can daunce
neither.[21]

When Rich talks of 'the measures' he is using the word specifically
but 'measure' was also a general term for any kind of dancing. At
the end of the instructions he has just written down, for instance,
Ashmole writes, 'Rowland Osborne taught me to dance these
measures', though only one of the eight dances he includes, 'The
Earle of Essix measure', has the exact title. Comparison of the
manuscript sources strongly suggests that the measures and the
pavan were one and the same, though there were clearly several
variations; the dances during a masque for instance, were usually,
perhaps always, specially choreographed but at the conclusion
when the masquers came down into the hall to dance with the
audience, they began with 'the measures', which must have been
known to those they took out as partners as well as to the performers
themselves.

Gentlemen at the Inns of Court, many of whom took part in
masques, had classes from individual teachers or attended dancing
schools, which seem to have grown more numerous in London
during the 1570s. An application for a monopoly on teaching in
1574 is supported by a statement claiming: 'There has late been a
great increase in the number of dancing-schools established; these
have been conducted by persons unqualified both by their knowledge and their morals, and have been set up in suspect places, to
which the most lewd persons resort. The Queen is particularly
anxious to suppress those who under the pretence of good exercise
entice the young to exercise lewd behaviour.'[22] Both the nobility
and the middle classes could have lessons in private, and in more
senses than one, to judge from the opening speeches of Thomas
Middleton's *A Chaste Maid in Cheapside* (1613); Maudlin
Yellowhammer, the ambitious goldsmith's wife, asks her daughter if
she has been with her dancing master lately, then launches into
sentimental reminiscence about her own youth:

When I was of your bord, he missed me not a night, I was kept at
it; I took delight to learn and he to teach me; pretty brown
gentleman, he took pleasure in my company . . .

(1. i. 14–17)

Clearly, Maudlin has close affinities with Chaucer's Wife of Bath,
who 'coude of that art the olde daunce'; later in the play she seduces
her son's willing tutor by inviting him into her 'husband's chamber'.

According to Leslie Hotson, 'to dance the beginning of the world'
was a euphemism for intercourse; if so, it is a singularly beautiful
one[23] which recalls not just a line from Antinous's persuasion of
Penelope in *Orchestra*, 'Dancing is love's proper exercise', but the
whole Pythagorean idea of the creation of life and order in the
universe, when 'dancing . . . began to be'.

Such philosophical ideas were of small or no account to those who
disapproved of dancing, the 'sad men' so gently alluded to by Elyot.
Among these, at least so far as the preparation of a prince for
kingship was concerned, were Erasmus and J. L. Vives, the Spanish
educationist who spent most of the years from 1523 to 1527 in
England. Writing of the occupations of a prince in periods of peace,
Erasmus lumps dancing in with other time-wasting activities:

How, then, can you expect that anyone who has spent his first
years among flatterers and frothy women, corrupted first by base
opinions and then by sensual pleasures, and wasting these years
engaged in gambling, dancing, and hunting, could later on be
happy in those duties the fulfillment of which requires the most
diligent thought?[24]

Vives wrote similarly in his *Linguae Latinae Exercitatio* (1539), a series
of dialogues on the education of a prince, which was immensely
popular during the sixteenth and seventeenth centuries; over a
hundred editions have been noted. It is dedicated to the boy who
became Philip II of Spain, who appears in Dialogue xx as the young
heir being given advice by a foolish counsellor, Macrobolus, and a
wise one, Sophobolus. Distressed to see Philip 'quite lean' with
studying so much, Macrobolus advises him to do

That which other nobles, princes, and rich men do – ride about,
chat with the daughters of your august mother, dance, learn the

art of bearing arms, play cards or ball, leap and run. Such, you see, are the studies in which young nobles most delight.[25]

In the final speech of the dialogue, Sophobolus sagely considers:

It is incumbent on youth, to reject and despise sluggishness, ease, little delicacies, and frivolity, whilst the whole mind should be intent on the study of letters and the cultivation of goodness of soul.[26]

The traditional Christian view that dancing is frivolous or worse, while not new in 1528, gained vigorous expression during the hundred years which followed. A moderate remonstrance is given in a translation of Peter Martyr's *Briefe Treatise Concerning the vse and abuse of Dauncing* (1580?) by I. K., who takes as his useful text a verse from Ecclesiasticus, one of the Apocryphal books, 'Use not the company of a woman that is a singer and a dancer: neither hear her lest thou be taken by her craftiness' (Ecclus. 9.4.). (The translation of the New English Bible has more zest – 'Do not keep company with a dancing girl, or you might be caught by her tricks'.) The same text is used as an epigraph by Christopher Fetherston for his *Dialogue agaynst light, lewde, and lasciuious dauncing* (1582).

The remarks of those who objected to dance on religious grounds range from the curious and imaginative to the impassioned and polemical. Dudley Fenner, for example, writes that the dancing together of men and women 'neyther agreeth with the shamefastnes of the one nor with the grauitie of the other. Nay, the very sight of it in a woman is founde to ouerwhelme men more then strong drinke' (Mark 6.22),[27] a reference to the dancing of Salome before Herod. Christopher Fetherston warns that he has 'hearde tell of those whiche haue daunced one halfe day for pleasure, and haue laide in bedde two whole dayes for payne'; after asking 'Call you this recreation?' he goes on to mention the diseases that follow dancing, which include broken legs.[28] But the majority of anti-Terpsichoreans seize upon the sexual aspects of dance, like the anonymous author of the *Treatise of Daunces* (1581) in the Lambeth Palace Library, who writes of the dancers' 'wordes, amorous deuises, or deuises of loue, wanton communications or speeches or markes onely knowen to the Ladye, or Gentlewoman' (sig. B7v). This is mild comment beside the fulminations of John Northbrooke, the thunderings of Stephen Gosson or the hysterical diatribe of

Philip Stubbes. Far from seeing the dance as a symbol of concord and harmony, this trio of Elizabethan wowsers portray it as the most pernicious iniquity of the age.[29] The extremists condemned all kinds of dancing except that which glorified the Lord. They quoted classical authorities against the art, and linked it with pagan idolatry and contemporary folk rituals of disguisings, maypoles, morris dancing, whitsun ales and pastoral festivals, so many of them connected in the past with fertility rites. For these critics the courtier displaying his agility in a galliard and the lady who took his hand in a pavan were no better than country Joan who came back from gathering may with a green gown and Jack who had helped her put the grass stains on it.

Dancing was continually associated with the theatre by the attacking Puritans, as the Oxford philosopher John Case acknowledged when he wrote in *The Praise of Musicke* (1586), 'I dare not speake of dauncing or theatr[ic]all spectacles, least I pull whole swarmes of enimies vpon me'.[30] One of these may well have been another Oxonian, John Rainoldes, whose *Ouerthrow of Stage-Plays* was first published in 1599. In a sober argument from Biblical and classical sources, Rainoldes comments on the unseemliness of men dancing 'like vnhonest women, like Herodias [sic], whereby what a flame of lust may be kindled in the hearts of men'.[31] His reference to Herodias, rather than her daughter, indicates the lack of Biblical example on which the anti-dance critics could draw; Herodias only suggested to Salome that she should ask for the head of John the Baptist as the reward for her dancing, which had so besotted her stepfather; she herself did not dance (see Mark 6.24).

The 'enimies' advanced on two main fronts: disguising was an insult to God, who had made man in his own image, and therefore acting, taking the part of another, especially a man taking the part of a woman, was sinful; dancing, unless it was in praise of the Lord, was also sinful. Even David made something of a fool of himself by dancing, perhaps naked, before the ark of the covenant, while Salome's infamous performance was the prime example of the wickedness of those who dance. The majority of Biblical references to dance, however, are commendatory, most of them referring to joyous dancing on occasions of exultation. John Lowin, Shakespeare's friend and contemporary in the King's Men, was able to write a defence of dancing on religious grounds in which he suggests that David may not in fact have been dancing before the ark of the covenant, as his movement could have been motion without measure (i.e. ordered rhythm), since 'his minde was transported and carried away'. Although it is entitled *Conclusions upon Dances, both of this age and the olde*, Lowin's brief tract is not a spirited effort, and unfortunately says virtually nothing about the dance of his day, apart from its value as a good exercise. In 1607 there was little heat in the subject anyway, for the players were flourishing, especially Lowin's own company, with its royal patronage, and puritan voices of protest were momentarily silent.

Perhaps because there is so little condemnation of dancing in the Bible, the religious reasons presented by the detractors tend to become lost in the welter of declamation against the lustful, lewd and lecherous results of men and women dancing together and the face-painting, wearing of finery and presentation of sinful acts on the (very unworthy) scaffold. Moreover, places of performance – playhouses, with their galleries, and inns with their upper rooms – were considered to offer invitations to sin. The Sabbatarian movement was gathering momentum at this time, too, and when the bear-baiting theatre at Paris Garden collapsed on 13 January 1583, John Field declared it an example of God's judgement against attending such places on Sunday. Over 1000 people were present and according to Field, who admittedly may have been a biased observer, one in three was injured, five men and two women were killed at the time, and several others died later.[32]

Despite such 'warnings' audiences continued to go to entertainments and the players and their dramatists went on to provide in the next few decades some of the finest plays ever written. By 1600 there were five public theatres around London: the Rose (1587), the Globe (1599) and the Swan (1595) on the Bankside, the Fortune (1600) on the western side of Finsbury Fields and the Curtain (1577) on the eastern. As well there were two indoor 'private' theatres, one in the Upper Frater of the dissolved Dominican Priory in the Blackfriars that was being used by the Children of the Queen's Chapel and at times by another boys' company, and another theatre of which the location is unknown, used by the Children of Paul's.

In all of these at some time dancing took place as part of a play or, at the least, in the public theatres in the form of a jig at the conclusion of a play. As an afterpiece, the jig was a stepdance in which the performers mimed the action of the song they were singing. Although few survive, it seems that many were bawdy; Shakespeare may have been showing his disfavour when Hamlet says that Polonius is 'for a jig, or a tale of bawdry, or he sleeps' (II. ii. 494),[33] but the epilogue to *2 Henry IV* was spoken by a dancer, and the possibility that he was the dancer of a jig cannot be ignored. It has been generally accepted that the German traveller Thomas Platter saw a jig after *Julius Caesar* at the Globe in 1599, but as the words he uses to describe the dancing, 'überausz zierlich' (extreme elegance) are inappropriate to a ribald stepdance, and would be far more suitable to one of the court dances, a pavan, almain, or even the faster coranto, it is doubtful that it was a jig he saw.[34] By 1612 post-play jigs had become notorious, and an order was issued suppressing them owing to the riotousness of the crowds at the Fortune, which, with the Curtain and the Red Bull, built in Clerkenwell in 1605, was especially associated with them. Jigs seem to have been extraneous to the action of the plays they followed, although one wonders if the actors ever took the opportunity to comment in their jig on the plot of the play just seen by the audience, or the relationships of the characters in it.

Music is known to have been performed before plays and musical interludes between acts are specified in some private theatre plays including Chapman's *Gentleman Usher* (1602), and John Marston's *Sophonisba* (1605), *The Fawn* (1605) and *The Malcontent* (1604), of which the last was also performed at the Globe. That there was sometimes dancing as well as music between the acts is clear from Beaumont's verse letter to Fletcher on *The Faithful Shepherdess* (1608), which mentions 'those, who, as the boy doth dance/Between the Acts, will censure the whole play', and from the stage directions at the end of Act III and during the interlude which precedes Act IV of those two playwrights' *Knight of the Burning Pestle* (1607), 'Music . . . Boy danceth'. What kind of dance the boy may have done is open to conjecture, but Platter gives a clue when he says he saw dancing after the manner of England and Ireland at the end of a play; this was probably at the Curtain. These were obviously folk dances, not the formal dances of the court which were influenced by the Continent. Writing about the same time as Platter, Robert Dallington commented that 'the French fashion of dancing is in most request with us'.[35]

Dancing as part of the action of plays was included in five principal ways. First, it could be an entertainment for other characters within the play, as it is in Lyly's *Campaspe* (v. i.), played by the boys of Paul's and the Chapel Royal before the Queen, probably at New Year 1584. This has little to do with the plot, but it provides an opportunity for the actors to display their talents in dancing as well as singing and acting. Dancing in masques within plays was at first simply part of the entertainment, as in Peele's *Arraignment of Paris* (1581–4), but it later became more sophisticated, so that the plot was furthered, usually tragically, as in Marston's *Antonio's Revenge* (c. 1600), a play for a boys' company, and *The Revenger's Tragedy* (c. 1607), given at the Globe by the King's Men.[36] A third use of dancing was for atmospheric effect, particularly to add to an air of festivity. In the first act of Heywood's *A Woman Killed with Kindness* (1603), for example, the wedding guests go off to formal dances in the hall, with chaffing about a dance tune, 'The Shaking of the Sheets' (which turns out to be ironic, as the bride is seduced into adultery during the course of the play), and in the next scene the audience sees the servants arguing over the dances they will have in the kitchen – 'The Hunting of the Fox', 'The Cushion Dance', and others with similar titles suitable for punning – until 'Sellenger's Round' is finally decided upon.

Sometimes dancing was included simply as an added entertainment and could have been omitted without damage to the play's fabric; the jig danced by Oberon and Bohan in the Induction to Greene's *James the Fourth* (c. 1590) is an example of this. But in many other plays the dance is firmly integrated with the action, as it is in Dekker's *Satiromastix* (1601) for instance, where a king's lust for the newly married bride of one of his subjects develops during a dance. The most beautiful and poignant use of dance in the whole period is in the last act of John Ford's *The Broken Heart* (1629), in which, during the course of a dance (most surely a pavan), the Princess Calantha is brought news, successively, of the deaths of her father, her friend and her lover. She continues from one change, one figure, to the next, stoically tranquil, but with her heart breaking within her. Calm, stately, marble-cool, the stage picture epitomises the themes of tragically restrained and frustrated passions that were peculiarly Ford's, and to which he gave a highly ritualised presentation. Finally, as the natural outcome of plot, dancing occurs at the end of some comedies as part of marriage festivities; Chapman's *Sir Giles Goosecap* (c. 1602), and Shakespeare's *Much Ado About Nothing* (c. 1598) are good examples.

The dances in Shakespeare's plays, like the songs, are all closely related to the dramatic structure both of the particular scenes in which they occur and of the complete plays. Dancing has a part in twelve plays certainly, fifteen probably. Directors often add them to others. There are only eight plays in which no mention is made of dancing in metaphoric, general or particular terms. From the beginning of his writing career in about 1590 to 1605 or 1606 Shakespeare brings dancing into only eight plays at most, but in the six years between 1607 and his retirement, from *Antony and Cleopatra* to *Henry VIII*, all but one or two, *Coriolanus*, and perhaps *Cymbeline*, contain dancing. The most obvious reason for this increase is the love of King James and his court for dancing and spectacle, the translation of the Lord Chamberlain's Men into the King's Men, and their enlarged number of court performances. Such reasoning, however attractive, must remain conjectural. But with Ben Jonson writing masques for the court and plays for the company, a king and queen who, however plain or ungainly, loved theatricals and believed in divinely ordained monarchy, an heir to the throne who was an accomplished dancer, and choreographers for royal masques who were so highly regarded that they sometimes commanded more in fees than either Inigo Jones the designer or Ben Jonson the writer,[37] then it is difficult to resist the thought that the amount of dancing in Shakespeare's later plays owes something to the influence of the court.[38] How his use of dance contributed to the articulation of his ideas, especially ideas concerned with order, is explored in the chapters which follow.

# 2 The History Plays and the Imagery of Dance

Therefore no dancing . . .

*Richard II* (III. iv. 9)

In the history plays to 1600 dance provides imagery, not action. The images are few and at first appear to be isolated, contributing most to their immediate context, but by accumulation they become part of a larger scheme which reaches its most complete form in *Henry V*. While minor in comparison with, for example, the garden imagery which has its most explicit visual expression in III. iv of *Richard II* and a fine verbal exposition in Burgundy's speech of *Henry V*, v. i, the imagery derived from dance is nevertheless persistent enough to enhance the audience's perception of character, situation and theme. Court dancing is the main source but Shakespeare draws as well on the morris dance and one of its associated characters, the festival king, linking war with revelry and with kingship, sometimes with one, most potently with both.

The first image of this kind makes a vivid connection between dancing and bloody warfare. At the end of Act III Scene i of *2 Henry VI* Richard, Duke of York, left alone on the stage, reveals the plotting of his insurrection, to be fomented by John Cade, the 'headstrong Kentishman' he has seduced to 'make commotion, as full well he can'. 'In Ireland', he says,

> have I seen this stubborn Cade
> Oppose himself against a troop of kerns,
> And fought so long till that his thighs with darts
> Were almost like a sharp-quill'd porpentine;
> And in the end being rescu'd, I have seen
> Him caper upright like a wild Morisco,
> Shaking the bloody darts as he his bells.

(III. i. 360–6)

The name 'Morisco' is more usually given to a dance than to a person but the word 'bells' in the next line makes clear that Shakespeare is referring to a morris dancer, the most familiar figure of English folk-dance. In the early sixteenth century the term 'morris' was given to a variety of group dances, but by Shakespeare's time it was also used with more special meaning, referring to the formal dance with its extra characters that has had such a revival in the twentieth century. A 'morisk' with dancers wearing bells is recorded as part of English court entertainment in 1515,[1] but it was in the country that morris dancing achieved its great popularity in the sixteenth and seventeenth centuries, often being associated with May-games. In a few places, particularly in Oxfordshire and neighbouring counties, it has genuinely survived to the present, retaining elements of ritual which probably owe their existence to pagan fertility rites.

Annotation of 'Morisco' in York's speech varies. Johnson gives a succinct definition, 'A Moor in a military dance, now called Morris, that is, a Moorish dance', which agrees in part with the entry for 'Morisque' in Cotgrave's *Dictionarie of the French and English Tongues* (1611), 'A Morris (or Moorish) daunce'; Johnson's is the only definition to include the connotation 'military'. James Boswell's variorum Shakespeare of 1821, which includes Johnson's note, gathers together evidence of morris dancing from the sixteenth to the nineteenth centuries. More recently, Andrew Cairncross's note in the New Arden edition describes the morris as 'a grotesque dance performed by persons in fantastic costumes, with bells attached to the legs, and usually representing characters from the Robin Hood legend'.[2] Even though its source is *O.E.D.*, this note is misleading; the dance itself, while vigorous, is often far from grotesque, being strictly patterned and carefully controlled.

The traditional six dancers wear elaborate clothing which differs in detail between regions (as the dances themselves do), but it can hardly be called 'fantastic', a description more fitting the dressing of the extra characters which frequently accompany the dancers. These can include a fool, a hobby-horse, a dragon, and a man-woman, sometimes referred to as the Moll or Maid Marian, and in some places now known as the Betty or Bessy. Today these characters are almost invariably danced by men, but in Shakespeare's time boys and women also took the role of Marian, one of the most extraordinary being 'old Meg of Goodwin the famous wench of Erdistan . . . she was threescore years (she saith) a

Maide, and twentie yeares otherwise, thats what you will, and hence hath beene thought fit to be a maide-marrian'.[3] The implication that Marian, and those who played her part, were less than genteel gives the substance to Falstaff's jibe at the unfortunate Mistress Quickly in Act III of *1 Henry IV*: 'for womanhood, Maid Marian may be the deputy's wife of the ward to thee' (III. iii. 114), that is, even the disreputable consort of Robin Hood, probably played by a man or a boy, would be a respectable woman compared to the hostess of the Boar's Head. This is the only time Shakespeare refers to the lady. Robin, Marian, and sometimes other personages from the Sherwood band, became increasingly associated with the morris during the sixteenth century,[4] but to say, as Cairncross does, that these extra characters were represented by dancers with bells is inaccurate.

The morris dancer's bells were, and are, his most notable items of dress;[5] they can be clearly seen in a contemporary illustration on the title page of *Kemps nine daies wonder. Performed in a daunce from London to Norwich* (1600) which shows Shakespeare's clown wearing a pad of bells below each knee to jingle with him all the way on his famous exploit. Beside him is a musician playing the pipe and tabor, the usual accompaniment for the morris at the time.

In saying he has seen Cade 'caper upright', York is using a technical term of morris dancing. The morris step itself is a springing on alternate feet, the dancer swinging the feet forward with the knees straight, while the caper, according to Cecil Sharp, is 'an ordinary morris step with an exaggerated spring; indeed the spring should be as high as possible, or as high as the time given by the music will allow'. He goes on, 'the springing leg must be in line with the body, which must be erect. The free leg is swung forward in the same way and as far as in the morris step, but no further. Some morris men habitually "shiver" the leg in the caper, that is, shake the free leg as described above'.[6] It is this last movement which is exactly described by York when he says he has seen Cade 'shaking the bloody darts as [the morris dancer shakes] his bells'. Curiously, however, it is Cade's thighs which are stuck with darts, whereas the morris dancer's bells are always apparently placed on the lower leg, between the knees and the ankles. Whether technically accurate or not, Shakespeare's description gains power from the contrast between the lively dancer and the bloodied soldier.

In the Oxfordshire village of Bampton the morris has a continuous history of some five hundred years as a Whitsuntide festival.

There, and at several other places in the same county, among them
Ascot-under-Wychwood and Ducklington, a cake is impaled on a
sword or stick and carried before the dancers when they process
from their meeting point to their place of performance. Cecil Sharp
plausibly suggests that this could be the survival of a pagan
sacrificial ceremony, the cake representing a cereal, rather than an
animal or human, sacrifice. E. K. Chambers comments that 'at
every agricultural festival . . . animal sacrifice may be assumed as
an element [and] the fertilization spirit was sacrificed at the village
festivals in its vegetable as well as in its animal form'.[7] The killing of
an animal continued to be part of the Whitsun festivals at
Kirtlington and Wychwood Forest, again in Oxfordshire, into the
nineteenth century.

A cake impaled on a morris dancer's sword is symbolic imagery
which has now lost its mystical potency. In the theatre, words can
convey a different kind of potency with a vivid immediacy, as they
do in *2 Henry VI*, IV. i, when Suffolk declares he would rather let his
head

> Stoop to the block than these knees bow to any
> Save to the God of heaven and to my king;
> And sooner dance upon a bloody pole
> Than stand uncover'd to the vulgar groom.
>
> (IV. i. 124–8)

Here is no animal or cereal sacrifice but a traitor's head borne on a
pole, a sacrifice, in a way, to the state. Suffolk's image becomes
visual reality in Act IV of the play when Lord Say and his son-in-law
Sir James Cromer are murdered and their heads carried on poles
through the London streets before Jack Cade's rabble. This incident
is of great dramatic importance, for the uprising has been
engineered by York. Leading his rout behind the impaled heads,
like unruly morris dancers behind a pair of Whitsun cakes, Cade is
met by Buckingham and Old Clifford, who persuade the crowd to
turn their eyes away from England to France, where preparations
for an attack on England are being made. Invoking the name of
Henry V, Clifford quickly wins over the mob and Cade flees, to be
decapitated in his turn by Iden, a loyal man of Kent. The head of
the historical Cade was itself set on a pole on London Bridge, along
with those of several other traitors, as was the custom from 1305 or
before until 1678.[8] Suffolk's image could have had a sobering reality

for those seeing the play who were wont to cross the Thames by the bridge,[9] and a head carried from the execution place to the bridge could very well appear to 'dance upon a bloody pole'.

It is not difficult to see Cade's followers as revellers – 'riot', interestingly, was a fifteenth-century meaning for 'revel' (*O.E.D.* sb.3) – and among Clifford's words to them,

> Is Cade the son of Henry the Fifth,
> That thus you do exclaim you'll go with him?
> Will he conduct you through the heart of France,
>
> (IV. viii. 33–5)

the last phrase is echoed and developed in *3 Henry VI*. When Edward Earl of March is on his bloody path to the throne, he declares during the tongue-lashing challenges before the gates of York that Henry V had

> . . . revell'd in the heart of France
> And tam'd the King, and made the Dauphin stoop.
>
> (II. ii. 150–1)

The word 'revell'd' turns the English wars with France into a series of feasts with music, song and dance. It is ironic that Edward is here using the same word, with a quite different emphasis, that has already been used by the unfortunate Duke of York in *2 Henry VI* when he is angrily lamenting the loss of the French lands; York likens to pirates those, including the King, who are giving France away to

> . . . purchase friends, and give to courtezans,
> Still revelling like lords till all be gone.
>
> (I. i. 218–19)

In *3 Henry VI* war and merriment are linked with deeper irony when news is brought to the French court that Edward, now king, has married Lady Elizabeth Grey, thus spurning the sister-in-law of the French King, who sends back to England the message that

> Lewis of France is sending over masquers
> To revel it with him and his new bride.
>
> (III. iii. 224–5)

Horrendous connections between singing and dancing, blood and death have already been made in Act I of the play, when Margaret is taunting the doomed York. Flourishing before him a napkin red with the blood of his young son, Rutland, who has been slain by Clifford, she jeers at him for withholding his tears:

> Why art thou patient, man? Thou shouldst be mad;
> And I to make thee mad do mock thee thus.
> Stamp, rave, and fret, that I may sing and dance.
>
> (I. iv. 89–91)

The idea of the mock king, that Shakespeare was to glance at in *Richard II* (IV. i. 260) and develop in *Henry V*, is here introduced when Margaret places a paper crown on her victim's head so that he is both a mock king and a 'king' who is mocked, viciously. The unlovely Queen's hellish nature grows to a new intensity as she then joins in the ritualistic stabbing to death of York, ending the scene with her Queen of Hearts cry, 'Off with his head'.

In contrast to the wider resonances of images linking war and revelry, morris dancers and bloody deaths, found in the early histories, imagery of the dance in the opening speech of *Richard III* most importantly illuminates the character of the speaker. For Richard, dance represents the effeteness of the court compared with manliness of the battlefield. The image, which is central to the speech, is introduced at the end of the second sentence:

> Now are our brows bound with victorious wreaths;
> Our bruised arms hung up for monuments;
> Our stern alarums chang'd to merry meetings,
> Our dreadful marches to delightful measures.

'Measures' is here used in the general sense of 'dances', and there is nothing in the words themselves to decry dancing; the actor's inflection – sarcasm, perhaps, or sneering bitterness – can however be a preparation for the scornful description in the ensuing lines of 'grim-visag'd war' capering 'nimbly in a lady's chamber'.[10] As his disgust grows, Richard, like the puritan denunciators of frivolity, links dancing and music with licence, speaking of 'the lascivious pleasing of a lute'. The idea of the dancing courtier, contrasted at first with the harsh image of the warrior, is then turned by Richard against himself; the sexual connotation is continued further and

scathingly connected with his own physical deformity. He is 'not
shap'd for sportive tricks' – a punning reference to both love-
making and dancing, since the elaborate steps of the galliard were
known as 'tricks' (Sir Andrew Aguecheek has 'the back-trick simply
as strong as any man in Illyria' (*Twelfth Night*, i. iii. 114) and
Guerrino in Marston's *The Malcontent* mentions a 'galliard trick-of-
twenty' (iv. ii. 8).) Nor is he 'made to court an amorous looking
glass'; instead, he is

> . . . rudely stamp'd, and want[s] love's majesty
> To strut before a wanton ambling nymph.

Shakespeare makes the same connection between dancing, ambling
and wantonness in Hamlet's tirade against women, delivered to
Ophelia, whom he has already addressed as 'Nymph': 'You jig and
amble, and you lisp, and nickname God's creatures, and make your
wantonness your ignorance' (*Hamlet*, iii. i. 146–7). The sense of
vulgarity is heightened here by 'jig', with its indecent connotations
stemming from the bawdy jigs performed as after-pieces to plays.

The content of Richard's speech then moves from indoors to
outside, from the easeful dalliance of the lady's chamber to the
'breathing world' into which he was sent before his time,

> Deform'd, unfinish'd . . .
> . . . scarce half made up,
> And that so lamely and unfashionable
> That dogs bark at me as I halt by them.

The dance image is still present behind 'lamely', with its double
meaning, and 'halt'; and the contrast between the courtly bower,
with its softly sounding lute, and the outside world with its yapping
curs is reinforced by the phrase 'this weak piping time of peace',
which calls to mind the shepherd's pipe and the pipe and tabor of
the morris and other dancing of the outdoors. Richard's dissatisfac-
tion with his body, the musical imagery and the first, punning
metaphor of 'this sun of York' are gathered together in the lines
ending this part of the speech,

> Why, I, in this weak piping time of peace,
> Have no delight to pass away the time,
> Unless to spy my shadow in the sun
> And descant on mine own deformity.

Since he 'cannot prove a lover', he is 'determined to prove a villain'; villainy is thus explicitly posed against love. Evil results in discord, love represents harmony, and throughout the soliloquy love, though degraded to lechery by Richard, has been characterised by dancing, the symbol of concord in the universe.

It is not surprising that a play which begins with a declaration of villainy has only one other reference to dancing, and that in a dull cliché. In Act III, when Richard's bid for the crown is gaining scant support from the crowd, he withdraws to another room on the advice of Buckingham, who then tells the newly-arrived Lord Mayor and citizens

> I dance attendance here;
> I think the Duke [i.e. Richard] will not be spoke withal.
>
> (III. vii. 56–7)

The meaning here is simply that of the *O.E.D.*'s '. . . stand waiting, or "kicking one's heels" in an antechamber' (*v.* dance 5); though it does not have the significance of the same phrase at *2 Henry VI*, I. iii. 170, it adds a further touch to Buckingham's character as a deceiver.

By the time he was writing *Richard II*, about 1595, Shakespeare had presumably come into contact with the court and had written *Love's Labour's Lost*, which contains twenty-two separate references to the dance, and *Romeo and Juliet*, his first play certainly to include practical dancing on the stage. Scholars usually place *Richard II* between *Romeo and Juliet* and *A Midsummer Night's Dream*, which has more dancing than any other Shakespearian play. The most courtly of the histories, *Richard II*, has no battle scenes, except those that are fought with words, and the elaborate formality of the joust in Act I Scene ii is broken off before the lances are even couched. It is both appropriate to this non-combatant quality of the play and an indication of Shakespeare's concern with the dance at this time that *Richard II* should contain more references to dance than any of the histories written earlier.

They begin with Gaunt's advice to the disconsolate Bolingbroke, exiled for six years by Richard, to take his sorrow lightly:

> Suppose the singing birds musicians,
> The grass whereon thou tread'st the presence strew'd,
> The flowers fair ladies, and thy steps no more
> Than a delightful measure or a dance.
>
> (I. iii. 288–91)

The use of 'measure' and 'dance' may appear tautological, since a measure *is* a dance, but Shakespeare was possibly thinking of the measure as slow and dignified and the dance as a faster, more agile display, or the measure as one completed part of a whole dance. In any case, Gaunt's attempt to conjure up a picture of civilised court life fails to cheer his embittered son for whom 'the apprehension of the good/Gives but the greater feeling to the worse' (I. iii. 300–1). This passage also includes the second of the garden images which, beginning with the Duchess of Gloucester's description of Edward's family as a vine in I. i, become an important structural element in the play, and are again connected with dance in III. iv.

All the images related to dancing in *Richard II* have negative rather than positive value. Mowbray, about to begin the abortive combat with Bolingbroke, declares that his 'dancing soul doth celebrate/This feast of battle with mine adversary' (I. iii. 91–2), for example. When the feckless Richard is in Ireland, and his supporters in England begin to desert him, the Welsh Captain tells Salisbury that he is leaving with his forces, since the omens suggest that Richard is dead:

> . . . lean-look'd prophets whisper fearful change;
> Rich men look sad, and ruffians dance and leap—
> The one in fear to lose what they enjoy,
> The other to enjoy by rage and war.
>
> (II. iv. 11–14)

The picture of ruffians dancing with joy at the prospect of war is a disagreeable contrast both to Gaunt's imagined gentle recreation and to the elegance of Richard's Queen and her ladies in the Duke of York's garden, where dancing is again spoken of. To the Queen's question as to how they shall amuse themselves to 'drive away the heavy thought of care', one of the ladies suggests 'Madam, we'll dance'. The queen sadly replies:

> My legs can keep no measure in delight,
> When my poor heart no measure keeps in grief;
> Therefore no dancing, girl; some other sport,
>
> (III. iv. 7–9)

one of Shakespeare's many puns on 'measure', and an ironic reflection of Gaunt's words to Bolingbroke. The whole scene is a development into a visual symbol of the play's garden imagery; the Queen's penultimate speech extends into a Biblical image of the first garden, which connects with the main religious theme of the play and its related imagery.[11]

Replying to the dejected Queen's angry questions about the King's downfall, the gardener tells her that in London the fortunes of Richard and Bolingbroke are being weighed. In the king's scale, he says, is 'nothing but himself, /And some few vanities that make him light', on Bolingbroke's side, as well as Bolingbroke himself, 'all the English peers, /And with that odds he weighs King Richard down'. The concept of the balance is echoed again in the next scene, but reversed, when Richard uses the image of buckets and a well to describe himself and Bolingbroke:

> . . . two buckets, filling one another;
> The emptier ever dancing in the air,
> The other down, unseen, and full of water.
>
> (IV. i. 185–7)

The lowered bucket is himself, full of grief, the dancing bucket is his opponent. The image of well-buckets for the vicissitudes of fortune is not uncommon,[12] but Shakespeare appears to have introduced the idea of the empty bucket dancing in the air. As elsewhere in the play, the connotations of 'dancing' lend ironic force to the word which is used in a profoundly negative situation. The image has a wide complexity of meaning. The bucket representing Richard is weighed down by tears, and dancing is inappropriate to sadness, as the 'weeping queen' of the previous scene has just shown us. Dancing 'in the air' could bring to the Elizabethan mind the sprightly galliard, reinforcing the contrast between the tearful Richard and the ascending Bolingbroke, but at the same time carrying the idea of lightness in the sense of insincerity – the implication suggested by Johnson when he considered that the best part of the comparison was the line in which Shakespeare makes the ursurper the *empty* bucket.

Images of dancing are used consistently in *Richard II*, and though not forming a major scheme compared with others discussed by Richard Altick in an influential article, 'Symphonic Imagery in *Richard II*',[13] they contribute to the remarkable coherence of tone which characterises this play among Shakespeare's up to the time it was written, especially the histories. By their negative quality, they

give expression to the theme of disorder which is such a strong
foundation of the play's thought and action.

   There are no references to dance in *1 Henry IV* and only one, the
Herald's unremarkable description of 'the dancing banners of the
French', in *King John* (ii. i. 308) but in *2 Henry IV* and *Henry V* dance
is associated either with the effeminate and the unwarlike or the
crude, as it had been, variously, in the earlier histories. In his
diatribe against Hal in iv. v, King Henry cries,

> Have you a ruffian that will swear, drink, dance,
> Revel the night, rob, murder, and commit
> The oldest sins the newest kind of ways?
>
> (iv. v. 125–7)

linking 'ruffian' and dancing as the Welsh captain had in *Richard II*.
The connection between dancing and youthful irresponsibility
made here by Henry IV is continued and developed in *Henry V*,
which gathers together the connections between war, revelry and
kingship which underlie the scattered images of dance in the
preceding histories. Dances of the court, the morris and its extra
character the mock king are invoked particularly to enlarge the
character of Henry V himself, and the way he is perceived by others,
especially the French. War is a major theme of the play and all but
one of the dance references promote the warrior image by
contrasting with it the picture of the soft courtly life of uncaring
pleasure, the 'silken dalliance' the chorus tells us is left lying in the
wardrobe while the youth of England goes to battle. Although
Castiglione and Ascham, among others, recommended dancing as
an accomplishment for noblemen, the attitudes expressed in *Henry V*
reflect rather the views of Erasmus and Vives, that dancing is a
frivolous pastime, unfit for a prince, and so the references to
dancing contribute to the presentation of Henry as the ideal
Christian ruler.[14]

   The dance images in this play both reflect on the character of the
young king and point up the contrast between him and the French,
especially the Dauphin. The first is the French Ambassador's
message to Henry that

> the Prince our master
> Says that you savour too much of your youth,
> And bids you be advis'd there's nought in France

That can be with a nimble galliard won;
You cannot revel into dukedoms there.

(I. i. 249–53)

This is Shakespeare's first use of the word 'galliard' and it at once shows how mistaken the Dauphin is in his estimation. Henry IV complained of his son's dancing with rough companions, revelling in the roistering sense, but since the Dauphin thinks Henry has carried over this irresponsibility into his political and court life, a court dance becomes appropriate for his sneering. At the same time, where King Henry's accusation suggests licence, the Ambassador's speech acknowledges, however mockingly, a certain prowess – a 'nimble galliard' implies a difficult dance done well. The image of war as merrymaking is then introduced to the play in a precise echo of Edward Earl of March's phrase that Henry V 'revell'd in the heart of France', already noted in *3 Henry VI*.

The idea of revelling is expanded in Act II Scene iv, in the Dauphin's reply to the panicking French King's order for arrangements to be made for defence against the approaching English; the Dauphin agrees that preparations should be made, but

<blockquote>
with no show of fear –
No, with no more than if we heard that England
Were busied with a Whitsun morris-dance;
For, my good liege, she is so idly king'd,
Her sceptre so fantastically borne
By a vain, giddy, shallow, humorous youth,
That fear attends her not.
</blockquote>

(II. iv. 23–9)

As well as ridiculing the English as a nation, the French Prince is lampooning Henry by implying that he is no more than a country bumpkin taking the part of a mock king in a summer festival. (Whitsuntide is still the traditional time for the morris in Bampton and elsewhere.) The festival king had many guises: the Lord of Misrule, the May lord, the lord of the Whitsun feasts, and the fool in the morris were some of them. In modern Oxfordshire the fool in his multi-coloured clothing is usually one of the best dancers; he is known as the 'Squire', and is often master of ceremonies. Cecil Sharp describes how he keeps the crowd back from the morris men with 'a short stick with a calf's tail at one end and a bladder attached to a string at the other . . . belabouring the wenches with the bladder and the men and boys with the tail'[15] – a sceptre 'fantastically borne' indeed.

A deeper irony is embedded in the Dauphin's implication that Henry is a make-believe May-game king, someone merely playing a role. The impression of irresponsibility the Prince gave when younger is only one of the more extended roles he plays during the course of the trilogy. His one role that is not a cover for something else, however, is the role of King of England. The perceptive Constable of France continues the idea behind the Dauphin's words when he says that the French Prince is mistaken, and that he should find Henry's

> vanities forespent
> Were but the outside of the Roman Brutus,
> Covering discretion with a coat of folly;
> As gardeners do with ordure hide those roots
> That shall first spring and be most delicate.
>
> (II. iv. 36–40)

It has often enough been commented upon that the play shows the effects of this change from the apparently frivolous Prince, more fit for a Whitsun game, to the responsible King; the Constable's speech carries the morris dance of the Dauphin's lines back much further than the multi-coloured coat of the fool in the morris, to the origin of the May-game in the spring fertility rituals.

The Dauphin has scornfully used an image drawn from the country to jeer at Henry, but it is court dances that supply imagery for the French themselves. After the fall of Harfleur, the French nobles try to call up their own flagging spirits; the Dauphin remarks that they are being mocked by their mistresses, who say they will give themselves to the English conquerors and breed up bastard warriors. The Duke of Britaine adds:

> They bid us to the English dancing-schools
> And teach lavoltas high and swift corantos,
> Saying our grace is only in our heels
> And that we are most lofty runaways.
>
> (III. v. 32–5)

The opposition between war and leisure, between the battlefield and the court, so aptly caught in Laurence Olivier's film of the play, is presented here more explicitly than it is in the French Ambassador's lines in the first scene. As the coranto is a swiftly moving dance, it illustrates well the idea of 'runaways', but there is an additional gibe in the reference to the volta, since in that dance the women are lifted high in the air by their partners. By calling their lords '*lofty* runaways' the French ladies are implying that they are effeminate as well as cowardly.

The opposition of hardened warrior and soft courtier first met with in terms of dance in *Richard III* is given final and explicit expression in Henry's wooing of Katherine in v. ii. Having demonstrated to the French nobles that they should indeed have taken their ladies' advice, since at Agincourt they showed themselves fitter for the dancing-school than for the battlefield, the English king now presents himself as the plain-speaking, down-to-earth soldier, incapable of the wooing niceties of the courtly lover. That this is only another piece of role-playing, like his roistering with Falstaff at the Boar's Head, or his disguise as a commoner on the eve of Agincourt, is clear from his last speech to Katherine before her father enters with the French and English lords (v. ii. 266–77). The pose gives Shakespeare another opportunity for punning:

> Marry, if you would put me to verses or to dance for your sake, Kate, why you undid me; for the one I have neither words nor measure, and for the other I have no strength in measure, yet a reasonable measure in strength.
>
> (v. ii. 132–6)

The speech and the scene with Katherine as a whole present yet another aspect of Henry, an aspect consistent with the development of his political character which has been apparent since Act 1 of *1 Henry IV*.

For the Elizabethans Henry V was primarily a military hero; Shakespeare's Henry is a complicated character who is, for instance, a warrior-king, a monarch with the common touch, a cunning politician, and a gauche Englishman when confronted with delicate French femininity. He is also a festival king, a mock king, a role-player; sneeringly described so by the Dauphin, and subtly presented so by Shakespeare, from the first scene in which he

appears to the last. In his soliloquy at the end of Act I Scene ii of
*1 Henry IV* Hal says

> If all the year were playing holidays,
> To sport would be as tedious as to work
>
> (I. ii. 197–8)

and goes on to declare his plan to behave as if all the year were
indeed to be spent 'playing holidays' so that his apparent reform-
ation, when he decides the time is right for it to come, will appear all
the more glorious. The connection between holiday and masking is
developed in Act II Scene iv, in which first Falstaff and then, so
much more successfully, Hal, pretend to be Hal's father; 'O Jesu',
says Mistress Quickly, as Falstaff assumes regality, 'he doth it as like
one of these harlotry players as ever I see!' (l. 385). When, as King
Henry IV, Hal banishes Falstaff, he is playing not only his father, but
ultimately himself as king. In *Henry V* he is the summation of the
mock kings Shakespeare has presented throughout the histories: the
wretched York, vilified by Queen Margaret, Jack Cade, Richard
II, who wishes himself 'a mockery king of snow' (but is it
Bolingbroke who is really the mock king?), Sir Walter Blunt, who
dies in *1 Henry IV*, because he is 'semblably furnish'd like the King
himself', and the six Richmonds who so confound Richard III on
Bosworth Field. These are epitomised in the Dauphin's jeering
implication that Henry is to be feared no more than a mock king, a
May lord.

The May lord, however named, was a fertility symbol, representing the birth of the new spring, and Henry partakes of this aspect of
the folk character in the final scene of *Henry V*, when he tells his
French princess (whom we have first met in a scene full of sexual
humour),

> If ever thou beest mine, Kate, as I have a saving faith within me
> tells me thou shalt, I get thee with scambling, and thou must
> therefore needs prove a good soldier-breeder. Shall not thou and
> I, between Saint Denis and Saint George, compound a boy, half
> French, half English . . .?
>
> (v. ii. 200–6)

As if to reinforce this facet to Henry the chorus gathers up the plant
imagery of the histories when he says

> Fortune made his sword;
> By which the world's best garden he achieved,
> And of it left his son imperial lord.
>
> (v. Chorus, 6–8)

In the character of Prince Hal–Henry V, Shakespeare develops the idea of the mock king dramatically to explore the meaning of kingship and to further his never-ceasing examination of the human personality. The mock king, the May lord, the Oxfordshire 'squire' are all aspects of one of the extra characters of the morris dance and Henry, who disclaims the courtly accomplishment of dancing, nevertheless embodies that character. He is the most completely evolved element of that line of imagery throughout the histories which begins with York's description of Jack Cade's 'capering upright' and shaking the darts that wound his thigh as a morris dancer shakes his bells. The lack of dancing itself in these history plays reflects their concern with war and disorder, but in *Henry V*, the last to be written, which concludes with a marriage and the prophecy of a birth and of political harmony (however temporary that harmony was to prove), dancing is mentioned more often than in any of the others. The final image of the play, moreover, connects King Henry with a garden, supporting the idea of Henry as a May lord, an icon of spring and fertility, who was at times the festival king of that most English of dances, the morris.

# 3 The Comedies I

Dauncing is Loves proper exercise.

Sir John Davies, *Orchestra*

Even if dancing itself has no place in the history plays, it could be expected in Shakespeare's comedies because most of them move from initial disorder to happy resolution and the dance offers such a strong visual image of concord. Several writers have noticed that the comedies themselves resemble dances in the balanced arrangement of their plots and the movements of their characters. For Helen Gardner, *Love's Labour's Lost*, for example, is 'a kind of ballet of lovers and fantastics, danced out in the King of Navarre's park'. Enid Welsford comments that *A Midsummer Night's Dream* 'is not a criticism of life but a dance, of which the underlying motif is harmony'. A. P. Rossiter finds that in *Much Ado About Nothing* the 'Messinans have dancing minds, and make words dance or caper'; the very movement of the dance in II. i, he says, is 'repeated and completed' by the play's action, 'and even the professed misogamists are dancing to the same tune'. John Russell Brown has remarked that in the early comedies 'dancing is the most eloquent stage action which Shakespeare used to celebrate a call to order and harmony';[1] this is true of *As You Like It* and *Much Ado About Nothing*, both of which end with a dance, and of *A Midsummer Night's Dream*, which has only two speeches after the last dance, but these are just three of the ten comedies written up to 1600. It may also be true of *Love's Labour's Lost*, but if so, it would be the only dance in the play, and there is no stage direction for it.

In the first three comedies references to dance are rare. *The Comedy of Errors* ignores it completely. In *The Taming of the Shrew* Petruchio talks of wealth as the 'burden' of his 'wooing-dance' (I. ii. 66) and Kate uses a current saying when she laments that she 'must dance bare-foot' on Bianca's wedding-day since she will be an unmarried elder sister of the bride (II. i. 33). But these allusions are unimportant. More interesting is an image in *The Two Gentlemen of*

*Verona*, where a few lines in Act III have a fantastic quality which accords well with the play's theme of transformation. When he is advising the Duke how Sylvia may be wooed for Thurio, Proteus suggests that the lady be courted with poetry and music:

> For Orpheus' lute was strung with poets' sinews,
> Whose golden touch could soften steel and stones,
> Make tigers tame, and huge leviathans
> Forsake unsounded deeps to dance on sands.
>
> (III. ii. 78–81)

The image emphasises the puniness of the foolish Thurio as well as having an ironic bearing on the speaker, whose classical namesake, the prophetic old man of the sea, used to emerge from the waves at midday to sleep on the shore; those wanting to learn the future had to seize him and hold him fast, a difficult task as he would change rapidly into innumerable different shapes. Only when he realised he could not escape would the prophet resume his usual form and agree to tell the future. While Shakespeare's Proteus talks of the monsters of the deep dancing on the sands, the mythical Proteus could almost be said to have performed a wild unruly dance when trying desperately to escape one of his captors (and in his dialogue on dancing Lucian satirically says he believes that Proteus was nothing but a good dancer); Shakespeare's Proteus changes his affections with comparable speed during the course of the play.

When at last he turns to dancing in comedy, with *Love's Labour's Lost*, Shakespeare approaches it cautiously, even flirtatiously, using the idea of the dance and specifically avoiding the dance itself. Much of the comedy of this play arises from the theme of the unfinished, the broken and the incomplete, which is an aspect of a larger concern with the recurrent Shakespearian theme of illusion and reality. An early statement of it is given in the King of Navarre's plan for a little academe, 'Still and contemplative in living art', announced in his opening speech. The scheme comes to nothing, in the first place because at least one of the proposed statutes is untenable even while it is being proclaimed, the condition

> that no woman shall come within a mile of my court . . . [and] if any man be seen to talk with a woman within the term of three years, he shall endure such public shame as the rest of the court can possibly devise.
>
> (I. i. 119–30)

Berowne points out that the Princess of France is about to arrive, a matter that the King had quite forgotten. Thus the seeds for the frustration of the endeavour are sown even before the play begins, and by an event outside the closed world that the men think they are creating.

This is the pattern of the play as a whole. Planned events which represent a turning away from reality are disrupted and foiled by the intrusion of reality. The most spectacular instance occurs at the end of the play when the show of the nine Worthies is broken up. There are two main reasons: the discrepancy between what the actors are and what they represent and the persistent interruption of the courtiers. When Costard is describing the show, the King wants to prevent its going forward but Berowne and the Princess persuade him to allow it; the Princess's words are virtually a text for the play itself:

> Their form confounded makes most form in mirth,
> When great things labouring perish in their birth.
>
> (v. ii. 517–18)

However it is the courtiers, especially Berowne and Boyet, who create the miscarriage of the piece and indeed urge on the hilarious quarrel between Armado and Costard which finally kills the entertainment.

A second, more serious, entry of reality comes with the appearance of Marcade and his announcement of the King of France's death. The whole play has been working towards this point and the intrusion here is one degree greater than the courtier's intrusion in the play of the nine Worthies because the courtiers themselves are in a world already removed from reality. The relationship of degrees of reality in this sense resembles the relationships in one of those intricately carved Chinese balls, which have one inside another, inside another and so on. Putting it another way, it is like a series of screens through which we and the characters can see. The final screen which the characters can reach, that furthest removed from us, is the most unreal. We, the audience, at the other extreme represent the form of reality most perceptible to ourselves.

When this idea is applied to the show of the nine Worthies, the low characters taking on the roles of Pompey, Hercules and the rest are seen to be at one remove from themselves; these roles are then shattered by the jibes of the courtiers who insist on the necessity for realism which is at odds with the illusion that the show is trying to

1. The moralising caption to this engraving of courtly grace and rustic vigour can be translated as 'Here flourish decency, integrity of behaviour, courtly charm, both grace and well-bred decorum. What wonder if divine qualities naturally follow divine beings. The bumpkin is as far from the courtier as the sheepcote from the palace – so much the uncouth dancing before you will show. But that's well enough: let the differences between different kinds of life appear as they are.' J. Th. Bry (1561 – 1623), from a woodcut by H. S. Beham (1500 – 50).

2a. Social dancing in the home, and dalliance of the kind which infuriated some Puritans. Attributed to Crispen de Passe de Oude, Dutch, c. 1600. (See pp. 12 – 13 and 60 – 61.)

2b. Morris dancers by the Thames at Richmond, with a hobby-horse, a female character and a bagman collecting donations. Detail from David Vinckeboon's 'The Thames at Richmond', early 17th century. (See pp. 18–21.)

3a. Woodcut from the title-page of *Kemps nine daies wonder, performed in a daunce from London to Norwich (1600),* showing William Kemp, the clown in the Lord Chamberlain's Men (1594 – 1600), wearing pads of Morris bells.

3b. A carole pictured in a fresco by Andrea da Firenze in the church of Santa Maria Novella, Florence; c. 1340. (See pp. 45 – 68.)

4b. A processional pavan at a Venetian ball. Giacomo Franco, late 16th century. (See, for example, pp. 5, 49–50.)

4a. Courtly ladies in a dance, probably a brawl. Anonymous French woodcut, possibly early 17th century. (See p. 38.)

5a. A dance, most probably a galliard, in a Venetian garden. Breu the Younger, Garden Festival in Venice (1539). (See especially pp. 5, 9, 58 – 9.)

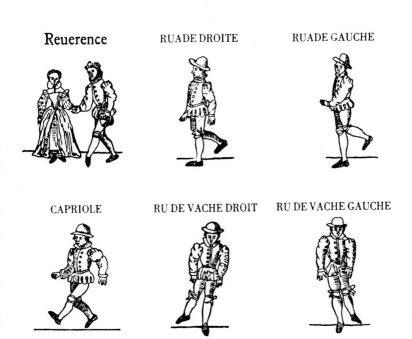

5b. Illustrations from Thoinot Arbeau, *Orchesography* (1589), showing the honour or reverence (see pp. 8, 97), and steps used in the galliard (see especially pp. 58 – 9).

6a. The volta danced at a courtly gathering. Note how the gentleman is lifting the lady with his knee as well as his arms. Anonymous French painting, late 16th century.

6b. Shepherds dancing a brawl. Anonymous French woodcut, late 16th century. (See pp. 38–9, 89.)

7a.  A processional pavan, livelier than usual, is led by musicians (see p. 85),
while a group of masquers with torch bearers and Turkish costume ascends
the dais, their leader holding a blind cupid on a leash. German (?) woodcut,
c. 1560.

7b.  Shepherds and shepherdesses dancing with bagpipes. Note that the two
who are dancing are crowned with garlands. English (?) MS, 16th century.
(See pp. 88 – 90.)

8a. Costume design for a knight or squire with an impresa shield for tilts or barriers at court. Inigo Jones. (See pp. 78 – 82.)

8b. Costume design for a naiad in Samuel Daniel's masque, *Tethys' Festival* (1610). Inigo Jones. (See pp. 99 – 100.)

8c. Two satyrs. Inigo Jones.

8d. Drawing of the descent of Jupiter in Aurelian Townsend's masque, *Tempe Restored* (1634). Inigo Jones. (See pp. 85 – 6.)

create. Nathaniel's nose stands too far to the right for him to be
Alexander, for instance. It is not just the courtiers who destroy the
illusion, however; a greater reality from the real existence of the
characters within the play breaks in – this is the life which has begun
two months earlier in Jaquenetta's belly. She is, as Costard
proclaims, 'Two months on her way' and Armado is the cause. The
news leads to a high point, perhaps for the Elizabethans the highest
point, of the play's merriment – the near duel between Armado and
Costard. At its climax Marcade enters, surely dressed in black, with
the news of death; and in eight short lines the course of the play is
devastatingly changed.

The illusory world of the show of Worthies has been broken into,
first by the courtiers and then by the initial reality, life, coming into
being in the world of the characters who are playing the Worthies.
Now Marcade's entry brings another reality; this time it is the final
reality, death, and this enters the world of the courtiers. It shows
them, and us the audience, that their world also is illusory and
artificial. As the play has demonstrated, it is a world in which oaths
can be broken, where deceit is a basis for relationships, even if in a
lighthearted way, and where love cannot be accepted as true
because it has not been tried.

The King, unsuccessfully, and then Berowne, with more success,
explain to the Princess that their love for the ladies has led them into
perjury but that the sin has been turned to grace by the love itself.
She makes it clear that the women did not take it all so seriously,
that they met the men's loves 'in their own fashion, like a
merriment'. The real world of life and death represented at these
two extremes by two offstage persons, the embryo within Jaquenetta
and the corpse of the old King, brings into the make-believe world
of the courtiers the conditions necessary for true love to exist – until
those conditions are fulfilled 'Jack hath not Jill'. These, moreover,
are the basic realities of our own lives so that the several worlds
shown to us during the course of the play are brought to a point
where ours can be included in them. The world of the play overflows
the stage and embraces ours, the audience's.

For the courtiers there can be no singing or dancing at the end of
*Love's Labour's Lost*, as the final harmony of their coming together is
postponed for twelve months and a day. It would, however, be
fitting for the low characters to end the play with a song and possibly
a dance, as Granville-Barker suggests.[2] Early in Act v Dull has said,
'I'll make one in a dance, or so; or I will play/On the tabor to the
Worthies, and let them dance the hay' (v. i. 133–4). Armado and

Costard have made up their quarrel and Armado has 'vowed to Jaquenetta to hold the plough for her sweet love three year'. Nevertheless the song is one of warning to the married and finishes with winter rather than spring, an indication of the hibernation of love before the springtime of its fulfilment. There is the sense here of life not incomplete any longer, but in suspension.

The theme of incompleteness is given its most theatrical presentation in the interruption of the show of Worthies, for this includes all the characters of the play, even those offstage, but the finale is led up to by a striking visual image of a dance which, while thoroughly prepared for, is broken off just as it is about to begin. Even though there is no dancing in the play except perhaps at the very end, the idea of dancing underlies the surface of the text; and it is invariably related to the comical. It is first mentioned by Moth at I. ii. 54 in connection with a dancing horse, a reference most probably to Master Banks's famous Morocco, 'a white horse which would doe wonderfull and strange things, as thease – wold in a company or prese tell how many peeces of money by hys foote were in a mans purce'[3] and many other tricks. Now at this point in the play Armado is telling Moth how he is in love, so that the slightly ridiculous spectacle of the dancing horse and the suggestions of trickery and charlatanism that go with it are closely, if indirectly, associated with love. The vulgar love and conversation of the low characters who leave the stage at the end of Act I are a foil for the delicacy and beauty of the Princess and her ladies who enter to begin Act II, and the entry of the men not long after is the signal for that dancing flow of words which so distinguishes this amongst Shakespeare's plays; it is attractively appropriate that the first words exchanged by Berowne and Rosaline are, 'Did not I dance with you in Brabant once?' (II. i. 113) (even if, as may be the case, these lines are an accidental survival from an early draft of the play). Specific dances are mentioned in Act III by Moth, again to Armado in connection with love:

*Moth.*     Master, will you win your love with a French brawl?
*Arm.*      How meanst thou? Brawling in French?
*Moth.*     No, my complete master; but to jig off a tune at the tongue's end, canary to it with your feet, humour it with turning up your eyelids . . .

(III. i. 7–13)

The French brawl was a very old dance, introduced to England in
the early sixteenth century, in which men and women joined hands
and danced in a ring, or longways; it was sometimes used to open a
ball. Some commentators think there may be a topical reference
here to the 1593 riots against the protestant refugees, especially
French Huguenots. Moth uses both 'jig' and 'canary' as very active
verbs; the canaries were a lively dance believed by the editors of the
*O. E. D.* to be of Spanish origin. In *Orchesography* Arbeau suggests
that it was derived from a dance devised for a court masque, the
steps being 'lively, yet strange and fantastic, resembling in large
measure the dances of savages'. Whatever their derivation, these
names are part of the word games of the play. All these dance
terms are again used in a conversation about love; and that extra
character of the morris dance, the hobby-horse, is good for some
bawdy punning a few lines further on. In the next act, Holofernes
uses a morris dance term when he tells Jaquenetta to 'trip and go my
sweet'. All these references prepare our ears and minds for the
gentlemen's assault on the ladies which is planned at the end of the
fourth act:

*Ber.*                    In the afternoon
                We will with some strange pastime solace them,
                Such as the shortness of the time can shape;
                For revels, dances, masks, and merry hours,
                Forerun fair Love, strewing her way with flowers.
*King.*          Away, away! No time shall be omitted
                That will betime, and may by us be fitted.
*Ber.*          Allons! Allons! Sow'd cockle reap'd no corn;
                And justice always whirls in equal measure.
                Light wenches may prove plagues to men forsworn;
                If so, our copper buys no better treasure.
                                            (IV. iii. 372–82)

In a play so full of punning, the close association of dance, time and
measure in this exchange makes it inevitable that the idea of
rhythmic movement as well as the idea of quantity should be
somewhere included in our perception of the word 'measure'. The
line can mean, for instance, justice whirls her sword so that she
metes out punishment equally, but also that she moves about with
an even, inexorable pace as in a dance. Berowne is sounding a
warning – since the men have broken their oaths they can expect

justice's sword to fall upon them. There is perhaps also some connection between justice who is blindfolded and impartial, and love who is also blindfolded, since it is because of love that the men have committed perjury, a point taken up again by Berowne at the end of the play.

Like so many other plans and projects in *Love's Labour's Lost*, the intended revels, dances and masks (i.e. masques) come to nothing, even if their frustration does lead to some 'merry hours'. Deceit is countered with deceit, invitation with decline. When Boyet brings to the ladies news of the plan to woo them, Rosaline asks the Princess, 'But shall we dance, if they desire us to't?', 'No', comes the reply, 'to the death we will not move a foot' (v. ii. 145–6). These words, spoken so lightheartedly, foreshadow the conclusion, for it is not until after the King's death has been announced that the Princess and her ladies are persuaded of the seriousness of the men's love and it will be possible for them to take part in love's exercise, even if it is twelve months later. When the courtiers approach in their Russian garb, their artificiality is at once shown up by Moth's mismanagement of his speech and then by the mockery of the disguised Rosaline with her continuing quibbles on the word 'measure', already previously introduced to us by Berowne. The measure, 'full of state and ancientry' as Beatrice says in *Much Ado About Nothing*, was the name used in England for dances to pavan music, slow and considered; and the King's claim to Rosaline that they have 'measur'd many miles,/To tread a measure with her on this grass' (v. ii. 184–5) indicates the basic seriousness of their purpose, which is being met with mockery by the women. It is mocked not only in words but in movement and, more importantly, in the lack of it. When Rosaline calls for music the King is not quick enough to begin the dance and she bewilders him by her refusal. When she does take hands a few lines further on it is to say farewell by a curtsy, which normally ends a dance. The Muscovites are mocked, the plan destroyed and in the process there is much merriment for the ladies and for the audience. Dismayed when the ladies later reveal that all was known to them, Berowne rejects the artificiality of 'taffeta phrases, silken terms precise' and tells Rosaline he will never more ask her to dance. In this he goes beyond what is necessary, as he does when he tells her in the same speech, 'My love to thee is sound, sans crack or flaw'; she asks him to leave off the affectation – 'sans "sans" I pray you'. His wit and judgement are better now than when he devised the masque of Muscovites, but they are still not so near perfection as they could be. That further maturity will come only after the twelve months he will spend among the sick, trying 'To move wild laughter in the throat of death' (v. ii. 843).

Like the planned academe, like the show of the Worthies, the dance is one of the 'great things' in the play that perishes at its birth. It fails because the ladies know the reality beyond the masks the men are wearing. From the disorder which comes from this knowledge and the ladies' refusal to dance comes the greater understanding of the men, and of the ladies themselves, and the deepening of Berowne's relationship with Rosaline. As well, we are prepared for the comparative solemnity of the last scene, with all the lovers, in which realities greater than any other in the play – life and death – break in upon the world of dancing words.

Shakespeare's flirtation with dance in comedy ended with *A Midsummer Night's Dream*. From avoiding dance altogether (always excepting the possibility of a concluding dance to *Love's Labour's Lost*), in *A Midsummer Night's Dream* he used it more abundantly than he was ever to do again. And he uses it deliberately to comment on and affect the major pattern of order and disorder in the action.

Dancing was a natural part of summer festivals and while it would be an exaggeration to claim that the May-games of the English countryside were the main inspiration of *A Midsummer Night's Dream*,[4] the spirit of the May-game, with its associations with love, licence and new life, is an essential part of the play's movement. Discordant notes of unruliness and irregularity in the world of men are sounded in the opening scene, Theseus remarking to Hippolyta

> I woo'd thee with my sword,
> And won thy love doing thee injuries,
>
> (i. i. 16–17)

but for these mature lovers the major conflict is over, the battle has been lost and won. Other violence soon breaks into the court, however, with Hermia's defiance of her father and his demand that she give up Lysander and marry Demetrius or be put to death. Happier disharmony appears in the second scene, when the artisans begin to prepare their interlude and Bottom wants to play all the parts. The malapropisms he distributes so freely reinforce the idea of disorder through their dislocation of language. These different kinds

of discord are confirmed and matched in the supernatural world of
the next scene, where Titania describes the foul disturbances of
nature which have resulted from her quarrel with Oberon. She
leaves no doubt that his rude interruption of her dancing with her
fairies is a highly important aspect of their dispute:

> . . . never, since the middle summer's spring,
> Met we on hill, in dale, forest, or mead,
> By paved fountain, or by rushy brook,
> Or in the beached margent of the sea,
> To dance our ringlets to the whistling wind,
> But with thy brawls thou hast disturb'd our sport.
> Therefore the winds, piping to us in vain,
> As in revenge, have suck'd up from the sea
> Contagious fogs; which, falling in the land,
> Hath every pelting river made so proud
> That they have overborne their continents.
>
> (II. i. 82–92)

The first mention of dance in the play comes after all four groups of
characters have been introduced – the courtiers, the lovers, the
artisans and the fairies – and the theme of disorder has been related
to each of them. Titania's speech, one of the great arias of the play,
summarises and enlarges the theatre of conflict. More is to come, for
Oberon, who has broken the 'ringlets' of the dancing fairies, that is
the perfect form of the circle, refuses Titania's conditional offer of
peace when she says

> If you will patiently dance in our round,
> And see our moonlight revels, go with us.
>
> (II. i. 140–1)

He scorns to join them unless he is given the Indian boy.

It is precisely appropriate that this quarrelsome couple and their
attendants are the characters in the play most concerned with
dancing for dancing was one of the main occupations of the
Elizabethan fairies. One seventeenth-century commentator,
Robert Kirk, remarks irresistibly on their 'paroxisms of antic
corybantic jollity'.[5] It was their principal means of getting from one
place to another. Shakespeare's fairies do not walk or run. They
'skip' (II. i. 61), they 'hop' (v. i. 383), they 'gambol' (III. i. 151),

they 'trip away' (v. i. 410). Flying was used for long distance and speed, and in one place seems to be synonymous with 'trip'; in Act IV when Oberon invites Titania, 'Trip we after night's shade' (IV. i. 93), she replies

> Come, my lord; and in our flight,
> Tell me how it came this night
> That I sleeping here was found
> With these mortals on the ground.
>
> (IV. i. 96–9)

Such constant lightness of movement is possible because of the fairies' weightlessness; Kirk refers to 'their bodies of congealed air'[6] and Titania wishes to 'purge' Bottom of his 'mortal grossness' so that he shall 'like an airy spirit go' (III. i. 146–7). It was just this effect of airy delicacy that the nineteenth-century romantic ballet tried to achieve when its dancers began using pointe shoes for the first time.

The dancing in *A Midsummer Night's Dream* may have been connected with an unknown occasion for which the play was perhaps written, the most popular view being that it was a wedding in some great house, whose singing boys were available to take part (though the earliest statement about its performance, made in 1600 on the title page of the first edition, says it was 'publicly acted').[7] Given the circumstances of having actors who could dance and sing, Shakespeare made dancing an essential part of the plot, a summarising action and a universal symbol instead of merely leaving it the delectable embellishment it might have been. The roundel and song which lull Titania asleep in II. ii, for instance, are a charm to keep away evil; they are no proof against the powers of Oberon.

The other characters who dance are the artisans, whose connection with the fairies' dancing is obliquely established when Puck leads in the assified Bottom saying, 'I'll follow you; I'll lead you about a round' (III. i. 96). 'Round' here implies a country dance, and Puck's meaning is a variation on the phrase 'to lead someone a dance'. The word 'round' has already been used by Titania in her offer of peace to Oberon, and it is picked up again in yet another sense when Oberon tells Puck how Titania has 'rounded/With coronet of fresh and fragrant flowers' the hairy temples of Bottom (IV. i. 48–9). Again the form of the ring is a focus of Oberon's attention, and here it becomes a reason for upbraiding his queen;

this time he is successful, and she gives him the Indian boy he so covets.

Then, Titania awakened and undeceived, Oberon calls for music and says:

> Come, my Queen, take hands with me,
> And rock the ground whereon these sleepers be.
> Now thou and I are new in amity,
> And will to-morrow midnight solemnly
> Dance in Duke Theseus' house triumphantly,
> And bless it to all fair prosperity.
>
> (IV. i. 82–7)

There is no direction given for when they are to dance; it is most likely after the phrase, 'whereon these sleepers be'. A full stop occurs here in all the early editions, and the dance clearly has two purposes. One is to ensure that the lovers and Bottom sleep well and wake refreshed – the dancers will 'rock the ground' as a mother rocks a cradle. The second, wider, meaning is to confirm the reconciliation of Titania and Oberon, and re-establish their domestic harmony. 'In every dance', wrote Sir Thomas Elyot, 'of a most ancient custom, there danceth together a man and a woman, holding each other by the hand or the arm, which betokeneth concord'.[8] Their dance completed, Oberon can say, with special significance in the first word, 'Now thou and I are new in amity', and they will therefore be able to carry out the rite of blessing Theseus' house on his wedding night.

It is not only Oberon and Titania who are 'new in amity' of course. The lovers are found in 'gentle concord' (IV. i. 140) and Bottom is soon to be reunited with his mates who had earlier fled from him. The jangling quarrels and jars in the play, however serious for the characters, have been for the audience like the baying of Hippolyta's hounds, 'so musical a discord, such sweet thunder' (IV. i. 115). Of this discord there is now only the verbal and humorous disjointedness of the interlude, *Pyramus and Thisbe*, to come, a sly comment on the earlier wranglings. Theseus sums up the paradox:

> Merry and tragical! tedious and brief!
> That is hot ice and wondrous strange snow.
> How shall we find the concord of this discord?
>
> (v. i. 58–60)

And to conclude, a bergomask between two of the company, a burlesque of the dance of Titania and Oberon in Act IV.

There is a double strand of humour here. A bergomask was originally a clumsy dance in ridiculous imitation of the movements of the peasants of Bergamo. Shakespeare has his clowns, already inept, performing a dance imitating the inept. It is the same kind of technique he uses in *The Winter's Tale* when Perdita, a princess in reality but unknown as such to everyone on the stage, dresses up as royalty for the sheep-shearing festival, and then is called by Camillo 'the queen of curds and cream' (IV. iv. 161). Bottom confuses his words as usual and asks if the audience wishes to 'see the Epilogue, or to hear a Bergomask dance' (V. i. 342); but in truth the dance may well have been heard, for it would have been done with stamping of feet, perhaps accompanied by the tongs and the bones that the metamorphosed Bottom had earlier requested from the fairies.

Their rustic dance, acrobatic perhaps, earthbound certainly, is the extreme contrast in the play between the mortal and the fairy worlds. It serves as an antimasque to the singing and dancing of the fairies which ends both the first night of the wedding festivities and the play itself. The words of Oberon again draw attention to the fairies' lightness when he tells them to 'hop as light as bird from brier' (V. i. 383). Titania's command, 'Hand in hand with fairy grace,/Will we sing, and bless this place' (V. i. 389–90), is a return to one of the oldest forms of dance, the carole, in which the dancers link hands and move to the music of a song, usually sung by themselves.[9] In medieval times the carole was used in religious ritual and in such ceremonies as blessing the bounds of the parish. The bringing of good luck to houses by the entry of singing dancers, hands linked, survives today as part of the May Day festivities at Padstow and Helston in Cornwall. The 'glimmering light' Oberon tells the fairies to give through the house hints at starlight, and the stars are a reminder of the heavenly harmony existing in the greater universe, so that in this way their dance widens out in its implications. Their grace and their ability to bless the palace and those within it bind together religion and fairy lore. 'Field dew' that can 'consecrate' is a striking indication of this fusion. By the time *A Midsummer Night's Dream* was written religious dancing had long been banished by the church in England, although as late as Henry VIII's reign dancing before the Christ Child on the altar may have been included as a part of Christmas ritual.[10] Shakespeare's fairies here take on the function of priests, both Hymeneal and Christian, with power to bless the rooms and their occupants, to sprinkle holy water and to prevent evil in the form of blemishes on mortal beauty. Their carole finished, they dance through the palace, carrying light and blessings.

Fairies also dance near the end of *The Merry Wives of Windsor*, but they are of mortal kind. Some are small – Parson Hugh's school-boys, commanded to 'Trib, trib' (v. iv. 1) – some are large – Parson Hugh himself, Pistol, 'Sweet Anne Page' and Mistress Quickly. Their purpose is benevolent – to cure Falstaff of lechery – but their means are mischievous. They model themselves on the fairies and hobgoblins described by Thomas Nashe in *The Terrors of the Night*:

> The Robbin-good-fellowes, Elfes, Fairies, Hobgoblins of our latter age, which idolatrous former daies and the fantastical world of Greece ycleaped *Fawnes, Satyres, Dryades & Hamadryades*, did most of their merry pranks in the Night. Then ground they malt, and had hempen shirts for their labours, daunst in rounds in greene meadowes, pincht maids in their sleep that swept not their houses cleane, and led poore trauellers out of their way notoriously.[11]

Pinching is a favourite means of tormenting and there are plenty of references to it in songs, plays and stories of the time.[12] These human 'fairies' of the *Merry Wives* dance around the oak, a tree with magical and sacred associations. And they are interrupted by the presence of 'a man of middle earth' (v. v. 78), Falstaff, who has unsuccessfully tried to hide his bulk merely by lying still on the ground. Now the fairies dance in a ring around him, recumbent like the defeated stag he is, performing their rite of purification. For that is what it is, however accusing it may be. At the beginning of their song, Falstaff is described as 'Corrupt, corrupt, and tainted in desire!' (v. v. 88), and although he does not make a speech of repentance, he does admit 'the guiltiness of my mind' (v. v. 120), and succumbs to his captors, saying 'Use me as you will' (v. v. 157).

The whole scene has the air of some pagan rite, with its oak tree, a man with stag horns, a wild rout of dancers and the expiation of guilt through mortification of the flesh.[13] This religious atmosphere gives a faintly serious underlining to the comedy of the situation. But it is only faint (though in *The Tempest* Caliban fears he will be 'pinched to death' as punishment for his mutiny against Prospero). Pinching is not a very painful torment and the tapers which touch

Falstaff's finger ends can do little harm compared with the torches of the witch burners. Then, when the trial is over, the fairies, the bringers of correction, disappear. The wild dancing and the actions with it bring the tangled threads of the plot to a satisfactory ending. Falstaff is cured, momentarily anyway, Ford is purged of his jealousy, and, under the cover of the dance, Dr Caius and Slender are deceived, along with Master Page and his wife, and Fenton can slip away with Anne to their midnight marriage.

As well as their part in resolving the plots of the play, the fairies in *The Merry Wives of Windsor* have a role related to an occasion, perhaps the first, on which the play was performed. Before they come upon Falstaff the fairy queen has a long speech of direction to the dancers:

> About, about;
> Search Windsor castle, elves, within and out;
> Strew good luck, ouphes, on every sacred room,
> That it may stand till the perpetual doom
> In state as wholesome as in state 'tis fit,
> Worthy the owner and the owner it.
> The several chairs of order look you scour
> With juice of balm and every precious flower;
> Each fair instalment, coat, and sev'ral crest,
> With loyal blazon, evermore be blest!
> And nightly, meadow-fairies, look you sing,
> Like to the Garter's compass, in a ring;
> Th' expressure that it bears, green let it be,
> More fertile-fresh than all the field to see;
> And 'Honi soit qui mal y pense' write
> In em'rald tufts, flow'rs purple, blue and white;
> Like sapphire, pearl, and rich embroidery,
> Buckled below fair knighthood's bending knee.
> Fairies use flow'rs for their charactery.
>
> (v. v. 53–71)

The first part of this is a command to carry out the same kind of ritual blessing of the house that comes at the end of *A Midsummer Night's Dream*. The second part plainly refers to a ceremony of creating knights of the garter. It is very likely then that the play was performed as the entertainment for such a ceremony and it is possible that the passage was added for such an occasion. There is a pleasant tradition that the play was written at Queen Elizabeth's command, 'and by her direction, and she was so eager to see it acted that she commanded it to be finished in fourteen days; and was afterwards . . . very well pleased at the Representation'.[14] It is an agreeable thought that the Queen's need for some lively entertainment after the solemn pomp of a garter ceremony resulted in this most domestic of all Shakespeare's plays. There was such a ceremony in 1593 but the more likely occasion was the feast of St George, patron saint of the Order, held on 23 and 24 April 1597 at the palace of Whitehall. Arguments for that celebration have been put forward by Leslie Hotson in his *Shakespeare versus Shallow* and more detail has been added to these by William Green in *Shakespeare's 'Merry Wives of Windsor'*. The closing scenes would certainly have made a joyously amusing end to a day of festivity and banqueting, although 1597 seems rather early. G. R. Hibbard ingeniously suggests that the fairy scene was salvaged from an entertainment for the Garter celebrations of that year and included in the play we now have, which must have been written at least two years later.[15]

As in *A Midsummer Night's Dream*, the dancing in *The Merry Wives of Windsor* is essential to the development of the plot, whatever the date of the play. As in *Love's Labour's Lost*, the dancing is closely connected with disguise, which is one expression of the idea of transformation in *The Merry Wives*. This is a more important theme in *The Two Gentlemen of Verona*, but in the later play Falstaff disguises himself physically, and Ford's jealousy transforms him into something of a monster, as well as turning him into 'Master Brook'. The attitude of Anne Page's parents to their daughter is distorted by their marriage designs for her and it is by disguise and the dance that she is able to frustrate their plans, fulfil her own, and present Fenton to them as an acceptable son-in-law.

# 4 The Comedies II

This marriage music hoists me from the ground.
Thomas Heywood, *A Woman Killed with Kindness* (I. i. 9)

The connections between dance and plot and dance and character relationships are developed with even greater sophistication in *Much Ado About Nothing*, in which disguise and deceit are used with more sinister purposes than in any of the plays so far discussed. Dancing occurs twice as part of the play's action, in the first scene of Act II and at the end of Act V. On the first occasion the dancers are masked and under this false cover Don Pedro woos Hero for Claudio. As in *Love's Labour's Lost* deceit leads to further complication. If truth had been the guide from the beginning, if Claudio had courted Hero himself, Don John would not have had the chance to plant the first inklings of doubt in the lover's heart. On the lighter level of the play this first dance allows for an exchange of wit between Balthasar and Margaret,[1] some straight comedy in the encounter between Ursula and old Antonio of the waggling head and dry hand and, finally, the scoring of Beatrice off Benedick.

The scene is structured so that the dialogue fits the movements of a dance, most conveniently one that is relatively slow, in duple time and with four or eight figures. A pavan is the obvious choice for the dance Shakespeare had in mind, for in that elegant perambulation the couples can be side by side with hands linked at arm's length and the steps involve turns back and forth, retreats and advances, so that it is ideal for highlighting dramatic conversation. The initial indication that it is a pavan is Don Pedro's invitation to Hero to 'walk about' with him – a just description of this dance. The ensuing fifty lines of dialogue fall into four units of similar length consisting of conversations between Don Pedro and Hero, Margaret and Balthasar, Ursula and Antonio and Benedick and Beatrice. These four units can be broken down further into groups of essentially four exchanges of line per partner and a concluding sentence. The lines are spoken as the dancers move, the meaning reinforced by the action. Hero, for example, tells Don Pedro, 'I am yours for the walk; and, especially, when I walk away', the second half of the line spoken as they retreat. He makes his reply, 'With me in your company?' as they come together again and she answers, 'I may say so when I please', as they take hands. This relationship of words and movement is matched by the next couple with Ursula's comment that she knows her partner is Antonio because 'Here's his dry hand up and down', that is, 'exactly'. From l. 120 to l. 135 the pattern is quite different, Beatrice giving a long description of Benedick ('the Prince's jester, a very dull fool', as she tells him to his masked face) broken only by the victim's lame attempt at wit. Beatrice concludes by saying, 'We must follow the leaders', Benedick replies, 'In every good thing', then Beatrice, as usual, has the last word, 'Nay, if they lead to any ill, I will leave them at the next turning', and there are two directions in the Quarto, 'Dance' then 'Xeunt'. What has clearly happened is that after they have danced their figure, with its accompanying eight lines of dialogue, they have become engrossed with each other, stopped dancing and just talked (or rather, Beatrice has). 'We must follow the leaders' could mean 'follow them offstage'; or it could mean 'Let us follow them in their dancing'. If there were a dance on the stage at this point, it could be a galliard, the quick, showy and energetic dance in triple time whose figures are based on five steps, which led to its alternative title of 'cinquepace'. That done, the dancers all leave and the stage is clear for Don John to start working his villainies on Claudio.

The pattern of the dialogue would suit several dances for which directions survive but the 'Madam Sicilla pavin' copied out by Elias Ashmole and now in the Bodleian Library[2] would be especially suitable, as it includes the partners' facing each other and taking hands and turning as well as moving side by side. It ends, moreover, with an embrace, which would chime particularly well with Don Pedro's last line, 'Speak low, if you speak love'. An analysis, even one so brief as this, shows how Shakespeare could use the movements of a particular dance form as a basis for dramatic structure. This scene also shows us another important aspect of dance in the play, that is the way in which it indicates character. From his conversation with Claudio at II. i. 136–50, it is evident that Don John is not wearing a mask and, just as obviously, he has not joined in the dancing. It would be inconsistent if he did, since the first greeting given to him is Conrade's, 'What the good-year, my lord! Why are you thus out of measure sad?' (I. iii. I). Being out of measure, he is out of step, as well as being sad 'beyond all measure'. His ill-humour brings discord into the play and it is not until harmony is restored at the end that dancing, unmasked and happy, can take place. Don John is full of the 'dumps so dull and heavy' referred to in Balthasar's song in II. iii. He is melancholy, a malcontent of few words, who has as his friend one born under Saturn, that sullen planet. He says, 'I am trusted with a muzzle and enfranchised with a clog; therefore I have decreed not to sing in my cage' (I. iii. 27–8). This dark, non-dancing villain is the play's extreme opposite to Beatrice, whose conversation itself not only dances but is also about dancing, as when she tells Hero:

> The fault will be in the music, cousin, if you be not wooed in good time. If the Prince be too important, tell him there is measure in every thing, and so dance out the answer. For, hear me, Hero: wooing, wedding, and repenting, is as a Scotch jig, a measure, and a cinquepace; the first suit is hot and hasty, like a Scotch jig, and full as fantastical; the wedding, mannerly modest, as a measure, full of state and ancientry; and then comes repentance, and, with his bad legs, falls into the cinquepace faster and faster, till he sink into his grave.
>
> (II. i. 58–67)

In this speech Shakespeare nicely prepares us for the dance scene which follows. It is not only in her own dancing that Beatrice is the opposite of Don John, who, as she says, gives her heartburn. While he refuses to sing in his cage, she is called by Benedick 'a rare parrot-teacher'. While Don John is 'not of many words' Beatrice is 'my lady Tongue'. He is melancholy, of the earth, she is surely of the sanguine humour, light, free and of the air, though not without a touch of choler. And when she was born a star danced. If Don John is in the 'dumps so dull and heavy' Beatrice is 'blithe and bonny' as the song has it. Their opposition is seen at its greatest in relation to Hero. It is Don John who fabricates the plot to betray Hero's honour. It is Beatrice who is her first and staunchest champion; who cries out the truth, 'O, on my soul, my cousin is belied!' (IV. i. 146) when everyone else has so far believed the illusion foisted on them by Don John, Claudio and Don Pedro.

As well as making this contribution to character, dance is useful for a little bawdy in the play. On Hero's wedding morning Margaret tells the downcast, 'stuff'd' Beatrice,

Clap's into 'Light o' love'; that goes without a burden.
Do you sing it, and I'll dance it.

To which Beatrice testily replies, with her mouth full of puns,

Ye light o' love with your heels! Then if your husband
have stables enough, you'll see he shall lack no barnes.

(III. iv. 37–42)

This conversation is echoed in the play's closing speeches when
Benedick, who has earlier rationalised his need to marry Beatrice
with 'The world must be peopled' (II. iii. 220), declares,

Let's have a dance ere we are married, that we may
lighten our own hearts and our wives' heels.

(v. iv. 113–15)

With Borachio and Conrade disposed of and Don John captured
while trying to flee the country, harmony is restored and the dance
can begin.

Dancing signalises the restoration of harmony of a different kind –
the return to health of a previously diseased body – in *All's Well
That Ends Well*. When Helena enters triumphantly with the King of
France after curing him of the illness which was believed beyond
hope of remedy, a stage direction is implicit in Lafeu's words, 'Why,
he's able to lead her a coranto' (II. iii. 40).[3] There is a special
significance in this line because the coranto is particularly lively.
Thomas Morley says it is danced with 'travising and running' and
Arbeau comments that the steps 'must be executed with a spring
which is not the case in the pavan or the basse dance',[4] even though
the basic pattern of the figures is similar. This joyful entrance has
been carefully prepared for by a series of dance references, all in the
second act, which move from a negative statement to this visually
striking affirmative. They begin with the sulky Bertram's complaint
that he is prevented from going to the Florentine war:

I shall stay here the forehorse to a smock,
Creaking my shoes on the plain masonry,
Till honour be bought up, and no sword worn
But one to dance with.

(II. i. 30–3)

Here he is bitterly comparing himself to a whore's pimp, soliciting custom, and to a fashionable dandy whose sword is merely a useless decoration of dress or to a fool or jester with a mock weapon. He sees his enforced confinement at court as equivalent to cowardice and, as in the history plays, dancing here contributes to an image which contrasts it with war and courage. Shakespeare had already used a similar image in *Titus Andronicus*: when Tamora's sons, Demetrius and Chiron, are quarrelling over Lavinia, Demetrius taunts his brother with

> Why, boy, although our mother, unadvis'd,
> Gave you a dancing-rapier by your side,
> Are you so desperate grown to threat your friends?
> Go to; have your lath glued within your sheath
> Till you know better how to handle it.
>
> (II. i. 38–42)

The reference to the impotent dress sword is jeering enough, but the strength of the insult is doubled with the mention of the fool's wooden sword, useless in itself as a weapon, which ought to be stuck fast in its scabbard. A charge of cowardice could hardly go farther.

In *All's Well*, Bertram is encouraged by Parolles to be less individual, to 'Use a more spacious ceremony to the noble lords . . . for they wear themselves in the cap of the time; . . . eat, speak, and move, under the influence of the most receiv'd star; and though the devil lead the measure, such are to be followed' (II. i. 47–54); 'the most receiv'd star' is the current fashion, and it is ironic that Parolles should be advising his master to follow the devil, who is leading the dance of fashion, when Bertram has just expressed his frustration by a reference to a fop's dancing-sword.

These negative images are replaced positively within the space of twenty lines when Lafeu brings to the ailing king news of

> a medicine
> That's able to breathe life into a stone,
> Quicken a rock, and make you dance canary
> With spritely fire and motion.
>
> (II. i. 71–4)

Lafeu's choice of the canary, more usually called the 'canaries', as an example, is nearly as extreme as his instance from nature, life breathed into a stone, for the dance was fast, extravagant and even wild in its movement.[5] In the next scene a more homely image from dance is slipped in among a list of similes used by Lavache, the Countess of Rousillon's fool, to describe the fitness of an answer that he says 'will serve all men' and all questions – the answer is as fit 'as Tib's rush for Tom's forefinger, as a pancake for Shrove Tuesday, a morris for Mayday . . .' (II. ii. 21–3). Although one among several, this image can be connected with the earlier discussion of Bertram and Parolles for it is part of a conversation which glances satirically at fashionable court manners. A morris is a fit dance for Lavache, a country clown, to mention, just as a coranto, a court dance, is suitable for the King to dance with Helena. Act II over, the play turns to battles and deceptions, and there is no more dancing or talk of it, even at the end.

A dance is called for at the end of *As You Like It*, however, when Duke Senior commands

> Play, music; and you brides and bridegrooms all,
> With measure heap'd in joy, to th'measures fall.
>
> (v. iv. 172–3)

Once again Shakespeare is making a pun but the invitation to dance the measures is more than just an occasion for witticism, an encouragement to dance, and a call to harmonious movement. Since the measures were especially dances of the court – among Touchstone's claims to good breeding is that he has 'trod a measure' (v. iv. 43) – the Duke's request indicates a return to the court after rural exile. It would be inappropriate to end this play with a country dance like the hay, for example.[6] The celebration is undoubtedly joyous, but it is also solemn, and the solemnity has been enhanced by the arrival of Hymen to present Rosalind and Celia to the Duke. Neither the realistic Messina of *Much Ado* nor the King of Navarre's park in *Love's Labour's Lost* could have accommodated such a figure as this marriage deity; *A Midsummer Night's Dream* has its own supernatural universe; but the forest of Arden is delicately poised between the real world, where survival is initially possible only by fleeing the threat of disaster, and the healing world which is Spenserian enough to contain green and gilded snakes and dangerous lionesses as well as religious old men who can convert wicked dukes to holiness. The last scene of the play is at the point of intersection of the natural and the non-natural, and Hymen includes both. His tone is religious, even liturgical – his entrance is accompanied by 'Still music', music that is soft and serious, and his lines are an austere contrast to Touchstone's catalogue of quarrelling which precedes them, a contrast which seems to be emphasised in Hymen's second speech:

> Peace ho! I bar confusion.

The confusions of plot have by now been resolved, but the mystical, the supernatural, and the holiness of love must bring the strange events to a conclusion. It is, of course, a conclusion which is also a beginning, for 'hymen peoples every town' – an excuse for marriage already noted as being used by Benedick.

The end of *As You Like It* is formal, with Jaques, already halfway to the conversion he decides to seek, distributing futures with a benign dignity of which he has given no earlier signs. He does not join the dance, he is 'for other than for dancing measures', and he is not returning to the world. Anne Barton has remarked that 'his absence from the dance sets up reverberations, asks questions more disturbing than any that were aroused earlier by his twice-told tales of transience and decay'.[7] Mrs Barton does not suggest what the questions might be, but there are good reasons why Jaques does not join the dance. Especially, it is because he is a melancholic; constitutionally, like Don John, of *Much Ado*, rather than temporarily, like Romeo (who does not dance at the Capulet's ball) or Richard II's Queen. More obviously, Jaques is not one of a pair of couples 'coming to the ark'. There is no partner for Jaques to hold by the hand or the arm, as Sir Thomas Elyot describes in his image of concord, and so it is inevitable that he should be gone from the scene when the lovers begin the dance, since it is presided over by Hymen, a deity of no significance for him. He may, as Mrs Barton says, separate himself firmly 'from that new society embodied in the dance',[8] but he too is going into a new society. The Forest of Arden has worked its transformation on Jaques as well as on the other characters.

The concluding dance in *As You Like It* is an image of harmony which both resolves the confusions of the play's action and indicates the hoped-for concord of marriage, though everyone, from Hymen down to Touchstone himself, would give Rosalind and Orlando a much greater chance of happiness than Touchstone and Audrey. It is both end and beginning, and the regularity of the movement is a visual reminder of that belief in the primacy of number which so fascinated the Renaissance. There are four couples in this dance, eight people, more dancers than at the end of any other Shakespearian comedy; the tetrad is of special importance in the Pythagorean theory of number for it provides a schema for the cosmos, while eight, as well as being a double tetrad, is the numerical basis of the diapason, the Pythagorean scale of notes made up of eight tones. For those aware of such ideas, this dance could have more than usual significance. In any case, its patterned movement is a comforting reinforcement to comedy's assurance that all is and will be right with the world, when our own experience so often tells us it is not.

Jaques, the reminder of real experience, shadows the sunlight of Arden, but while difficulties are suggested in *As You Like It*, in *Twelfth Night* uncertainty, ambiguity, near-madness and disorder give an altogether darker tone to the play. Although there is a resolution at the end, there is no dancing. Two couples are on the stage, the newly wed Olivia and Sebastian, and Viola and Orsino, but Viola is still Cesario, and 'shall be while [she is] a man'; not until she is seen in other habits can she become 'Orsino's mistress, and his fancy's queen'. Finally, the stage is left to Feste, whose song is harsh, with 'the words of Mercury' to borrow Armado's concluding phrase from *Love's Labour's Lost*, not the music of Apollo. The opposition of these two gods is the opposition of death and life, for Mercury conducted the souls of the dead to the coldness of Pluto's kingdom, and one of the first acts of Apollo, god of warmth and sunlight, was the defeat at Delphi of Python, the dragon who represented the dark forces of the underworld. The melody may do something to mitigate the bleak meaning of Feste's song, which depicts a drunkard's progress to the point where, cast out of the society of men, he must seek a bed where he can; when you have sunk to this degree, it may well indeed appear that the rain 'raineth every day'.[9]

It is an ending which Sir Toby Belch may yet escape, though he is threatened. In Act II his carousing is invaded by Malvolio:

> Sir Toby, I must be round with you. My lady bade me tell you that, though she harbours you as her kinsman, she's nothing allied to your disorders. If you can separate yourself and your misdemeanours, you are welcome to the house; if not, and it would please you to take leave of her, she is very willing to bid you farewell.
>
> (II. iii. 91–6)

It is one of the play's more subtle ironies that all the references to dancing in it are given to Sir Toby and Sir Andrew Aguecheek, a drunkard and a fool; most of them occur in one scene, their first scene together, I. iii.

| | |
|---|---|
| *Sir And.* | . . . I would I had bestowed that time in the tongues that I have in fencing, dancing, and bear-baiting. O, had I but followed the arts! |
| | . . . I am a fellow o' th' strangest mind i' th' world; I delight in masques and revels sometimes altogether. |
| *Sir To.* | Art thou good at these kick-shawses, knight? |
| *Sir And.* | As any man in Illyria, whatsoever he be, under the degree of my betters; and yet I will not compare with an old man. |
| *Sir To.* | What is thy excellence in a galliard, knight? |
| *Sir And.* | Faith, I can cut a caper. |
| *Sir To.* | And I can cut the mutton to't. |
| *Sir And.* | And I think I have the back-trick simply as strong as any man in Illyria. |
| *Sir To.* | Wherefore are these things hid? . . . Why dost thou not go to church in a galliard and come home in a coranto? My very walk should be a jig; I would not so much as make water but in a sink-a-pace. What dost thou mean? Is it a world to hide virtues in? I did think, by the excellent constitution of thy leg, it was form'd under the star of a galliard. |
| *Sir And.* | Ay, 'tis strong, and it does indifferent well in a flame-colour'd stock. Shall we set about some revels? |
| *Sir To.* | What shall we do else? Were we not born under Taurus? |
| *Sir And.* | Taurus? That's sides and heart. |
| *Sir To.* | No, sir; it is legs and thighs. Let me see thee caper. Ha, higher! Ha, ha, excellent! |

(I. iii. 87–133)

R. A. Foakes sees Sir Toby as one of the voices of maturity in the play, 'the effective centre of a group consisting of Maria, Fabian, Feste, and Sir Andrew',[10] and to an extent that view is supported by this conversation, which sketches a background for the two knights which separates them from the Illyrian world around them. It represents them as courtiers educated in some of the gentlemanly accomplishments of the sixteenth century. Sir Andrew, characteristically, has just missed out – fencing, dancing and music, not bear-baiting, were the courtly trivium;[11] bear-baiting was a spectacular sport though, popular among the courtiers.

Sir Toby and Sir Andrew, then, are presented in this passage as gentlemen of courtly attainments – but courtly attainments undoubtedly gone to seed. The 'foolish knight' is being somewhat wistful when he says that he delights in 'masques and revels sometimes altogether'. Sir Toby makes fun of him over the very matter on which he has expressed regret – his dancing – and the loaded question about his excellence in a galliard is especially barbed, for the galliard, according to Arbeau, 'is so called because one must be gay and nimble to dance it, as, even when performed reasonably slowly, the movements are light-hearted. And it needs must be slower for a man of large stature than for a small man, inasmuch as the tall one takes longer to execute his steps and in moving his feet backwards and forwards than the short one'. Moreover, he tells his pupil, Capriol, the steps and movements of the galliard 'are quick and gay, so that young men of your age are better suited to dance them than old ones like myself'.[12] Sir Andrew is not an old man, unless Sir Toby is being heavily satirical when he indicates that Orsino is much older (1. iii. 104–6), but his association with Sir Toby inclines one to think of him as more than a mere youth; the irony would have more point if this were the case. As well, the galliard is the most showy of dances, in which the man exhibits his graceful agility to his partner, or sometimes as a soloist. Among the steps he could perform are a rapid crossing and uncrossing of the feet, known as a fleuret, and a high leap in which the dancer makes two revolutions in the air before landing lightly on his two feet with his knees slightly bent, to give a better grace and avoid thumping heavily on the floor – what became in classical ballet a *double tour en l'air*. The imagined picture of Sir Andrew executing such a feat is funny enough in itself.

Sir Toby takes up Sir Andrew's answer that he can 'cut a caper' by replying in terms of mutton and caper sauce, but adds a further spice of bawdry. 'Mutton' was, of course, a cant term for a whore, so that Sir Andrew's innocent remark that he thinks he has 'the backtrick simply as strong as any man in Illyria' takes on a bawdy meaning. What he is so proud of, however, is not his sexual prowess, but his ability to perform a dance movement, probably the ruade step in the galliard, in which the dancer kicks his foot behind him. Sir Toby continues to make fun of him – if he can dance so well, then, he asks, why doesn't he go to church dancing a quick dance, a galliard, and return dancing an even quicker one, a coranto (Arbeau talks of a coranto danced 'helter-skelter').

A jig is vulgar company for these other, courtly, dances. But Sir Toby lowers the dignity of the cinquepace by making a pun about urination, which perhaps shows the level at which he thinks about Sir Andrew, whose leg, he goes on flatteringly to say, must have been 'form'd under the star of a galliard' (i.e. a cinquepace). And Sir Andrew falls into the trap once more; Taurus is the sign neither for sides and heart nor legs and thighs – it governs the neck and throat – but it allows another suggestive comment from Sir Toby and further ridicule of Sir Andrew, this time visual, as the unfortunate innocent capers ever higher in the air at his tormenter's command, demonstrating both his excellence (or lack of it) in a galliard and his willing gullibility.

Just as Sir Andrew is the victim in this small scene, so he is deceived on a larger scale about his prospects as a suitor to Olivia by Sir Toby, who is using him as a source of drink and money; when Fabian says of Sir Andrew in Act III, 'This is a dear manakin to you, Sir Toby', Toby replies, 'I have been dear to him, lad – some two thousand strong, or so' (III. ii. 49–51). And Aguecheek is probably deceived to the end – though he has good reason to perceive Sir Toby's real attitude in the drunken knight's last line in the play. After they have both been trounced by Sebastian, whom they have mistaken for Cesario–Viola, the two enter with bloody, broken heads. Sir Andrew, still unaware, supports Sir Toby, saying of their supposed adversary, 'if he had not been in drink, he would have tickl'd you othergates than he did'; but when he says 'I'll help you, Sir Toby, because we'll be dress'd together', the wounded Belch viciously turns on him: 'Will you help – an ass-head and a coxcomb and a knave, a thin fac'd knave, a gull?' (v. i. 185, 196–9). No joy, no harmony here.

The debasement to which Sir Toby has fallen is indicated by a reference to dance which has puzzled many commentators. 'Sot', he says to Feste, 'didst see Dick Surgeon, sot?' 'O, he's drunk, Sir Toby – an hour agone,' is the answer; 'his eyes were set at eight i' th' morning'. This ironic reflection on Sir Toby's earlier remark that 'to go to bed after midnight is to go to bed betimes' (II. iii. 7) is now taken up by him in an entirely different way – 'Then he's a rogue and a passy measures pavin', he says. 'I hate a drunken rogue'. (The confusion is compounded by the Folio text, which reads 'panyn' for 'pavin', but the latter reading is now generally accepted.) The passing measures pavan was a dance performed to music known as *passamezzo antico*, in which the melody was played over a base tune of long notes, each of which corresponded to a step unit of the dance;[13] the dance and the music are thus more than usually unified. Toby's insult has been triggered off by Feste's comment that the eyes of the surgeon, who should be awake and available to minister aid to the injured, 'were set at eight i' th' morning' (set, presumably, as the sun sets at night). It may be that Sir Toby's brain picks up the number eight[14] and connects it with the pavan – Thomas Morley comments that the pavan consists of three strains, each of eight, twelve, or sixteen semibreves, and 'fewer than eight I have not seen' – but the greatest value of Sir Toby's remark lies in its irony. When his own life is so disordered he uses, as an insult, the name of a dance which was an example of exceptionally unified concord.

Sir Toby has had one other reference to dancing, and it is, again, deeply ironic. As he, Sir Andrew and Feste are settling into their drunken revelry in II. iii, he asks, 'But shall we make the welkin dance indeed? Shall we rouse the night-owl in a catch that will draw three souls out of one weaver? Shall we do that?' (II. iii. 56–8). He is merely calling for a rousing chorus, loud enough to reach the skies and move them to dance. But to make the welkin dance, to have the sky dancing, would be to have the stars, the planets and the spheres moving together in a harmony and order which would be mirrored on the earth beneath. The result of their carousing, however, is to bring immediate hostility, disorder and confusion, since the steward's admonition leads to Maria's plot with the forged letter, the yellow stockings and cross garters, the confinement of Malvolio and his eventual vow of revenge on the whole pack of them.

Maria's news that sometimes Malvolio is 'a kind of Puritan' (II. iii. 132) intensifies the division between him and the revellers. It is possible that Leslie Hotson is right in his claim that Malvolio satirises the puritan Comptroller of the Queen's household, Sir William Knollys,[15] but even if that were not so, an Elizabethan audience would have been at least aware of, and at best familiar with, some of the more passionate denunciations of dance from puritan polemicists like Philip Stubbes, who declared in 1583:

> Dauncing, as it is vsed (or rather abused) in these daies, is an introduction to whordom, a preparatiue to wantonnes, a pro- uocative to vncleanes, & an introite to al kind of lewdenes,

rather than a pleasant exercyse to the mind, or a holsome practise
for the body: yet, notwithstanding . . . men, wemen, & children,
are so skilful in this laudable science, as they maye be thought
nothing inferiour to Cynoedus, the prostitut ribauld, nor yet to
Sardanapalus, that effeminate varlet. Yea, thei are not ashamed
to erect scholes of dauncing, thinking it an ornament to their
children to be expert in this noble science of heathen
diuelrie. . . . For what clipping, what culling, what kissing and
bussing, what smouching & slabbering one of another, what
filthie groping and vncleane handling is not practised euery wher
in these dauncings? . . . But, say they, it induceth looue: so I say
also; but what looue? Truely, a lustful looue, a venereous looue, a
concupiscencious, baudie, & beastiall looue, such as pro-
ceedeth from the stinking pump and lothsome sink of carnall
affection and fleshly appetite, and not such as distilleth from the
bowels of the hart ingenerat by the spirit of God.[16]

To be so emotionally virtuous as this is to be a little mad, and would
not be out of place in Illyria.

Sir Toby and his topers may represent voices of maturity, as R. A.
Foakes suggests, but it is a maturity that has gone bad. Sir Toby's
wit has turned to gulling an innocent so that the guller can indulge
his own drunkenness. His courtliness has decayed, the accomplishment of dancing become fodder for bawdy jokes and petulant abuse.
He is a representative of a fallen world – and this is physically
represented on stage, vividly, in his being wounded by Sebastian, a
man come from outside Illyria, who administers a strong dose of
reality to begin the new world in the play. Not that this new world
will be so golden as the world we are entering at the end of *As You
Like It*. The conclusion of *Twelfth Night*, whose lord of Misrule is
finally crowned with a bloody pate, is toned to the words of
Mercury. And there is no dancing any more than at the end of *All's
Well that Ends Well*, which concludes some little time after the
marriage of Helena and Bertram, and with an equivocal, conditional couplet by the King,

> All yet seems well; and if it end so meet,
> The bitter past, more welcome is the sweet.
>
> (v. iii. 326–7)[17]

*As You Like It*, like *Much Ado About Nothing*, ends more in tune with the songs of Apollo. Hymen traditionally wore yellow, the colour of the sun, and Apollo, patron of the Muses, would have looked benevolently on the dancing, which signifies present concord and future harmony, at the conclusion of those plays.

# 5 The Tragedies

> The black soft-footed hour is now on wing,
> Which, for my wreak, ghosts shall celebrate
> With dances dire and infernal state.
>
> George Chapman, *The Revenge of Bussy D'Ambois*
> (v. iii. 55–7)

In Elizabethan and Jacobean tragedy dancing is usually connected with death. John Marston, for instance, presents an elaborate, ritualised killing as the climax of a dance in *Antonio's Revenge* (*c.* 1600); in *The Revenger's Tragedy* (1607) a group of masked dancers reveal themselves as murderers; in John Ford's *'Tis Pity She's a Whore* (*c.* 1628) the jealous Hippolyta tries to poison her former lover Soranzo during the course of a dance, only to have her plot foiled so that she dies instead. In the lurid Italianate world of these plays dancing, at odds with its true significance, is a concealment for evil. In *Romeo and Juliet*, possibly the first play in which Shakespeare introduces dancing into the action, it is not used as a disguise for evil but is closely and ominously connected with it.

The first mention of dance is light-hearted enough, with the punning that is typical of the play, but the tone is strongly negative. Romeo's friends are persuading him to go with them to the Capulet's feast when Benvolio, sharing some wordplay with Berowne, says

> let them measure us by what they will,
> We'll measure them a measure, and be gone.
> (i. iv. 9–10)

Romeo, unhappy in his love for the scornful Rosaline, will not go to dance. His friends may have 'dancing shoes/With nimble soles', he is bound to the earth by a 'soul of lead', but he agrees to go with them as a torchbearer.

Benvolio's 'measure' is given form in the next scene by the

dancers at the feast. Having seen Juliet among them, and so suddenly fallen in love, Romeo says, 'The measure done, I'll watch her place of stand' (I. v. 48). Benvolio was using the word as a general term for a dance – 'we'll show them how we can do a dance, and then be off' – Romeo is using it in the sense of a part of a dance, in Italy part of a *ballo*, a dance consisting of several figures in different rhythms. There might be, for instance, a figure for all the dancers, followed by one for the women alone, then one for the men, and one in which groups of two men and one woman would dance together. Such a figure as this last is in fact described by Luigi da Porto in his version of the Romeo and Juliet story, which Shakespeare may have known; there, Juliet dances with Mercutio on one side and Romeo on the other, each taking one of her hands.[1] Shakespeare's Romeo does not dance, but waits for Juliet to finish the figure. She comes to him out of the dance, the symbol of harmony, which probably continues behind them; they meet, speak and kiss against a background of dance and music. This powerfully metaphysical ambience enhances the supremely important moment; it also provides a strong ironic contrast to the discord and tragedy which follow. The lovers are still, having no part in the regular movement, and when Juliet soon after identifies Romeo to the Nurse as 'he . . . that would not dance' (I. v. 130), their isolation from the pattern of order is further reinforced. The dancing, however, also visually echoes the perception of beauty and the birth of love. Romeo declares that he 'ne'er saw true beauty till this night' (I. v. 51); Ficino speaks of love's circular motion and its connection with beauty. The 'divine quality of beauty stirs desire for itself in all things: and that is love. The world that was originally drawn out of God is thus drawn back to God; there is a continual attraction between them . . . moving as it were in a circle'.[2] Shakespeare emphasises the divine quality of Romeo and Juliet's love by his use of dance as a prelude and a background to its revelation, by the wordplay on 'pilgrim', 'palm' and 'palmer', perhaps by Romeo's disguise as a holy man (though if he is wearing disguise it is insufficient to hide him from Tybalt and Capulet) and by the kisses exchanged by the lovers. Framed as they are in talk of sin, faith and prayer, these kisses evoke the idea of a kiss being 'rather a coupling together of the soul, than of the body'.[3]

The background of movement to this whole sequence, from Romeo's first sight of Juliet to their kiss (I. v. 40–108) is a physical expression of that wider scheme of celestial imagery and imagery of light and dark in the play which has been commented upon in the past.[4] It is also intimately connected with love. For Lucian, 'dance came into being contemporaneously with Love',[5] an idea from which Davies made his exquisite *Orchestra*. Lucian continues by speaking of 'the concord of the heavenly spheres, the interlacing of the errant planets with the fixed stars, their rhythmic agreement and timed harmony'. An impression of 'errant planets and fixed stars', 'rhythmic agreement and timed harmony', can be given on the stage by torches held aloft by the men as they dance. Da Porto speaks of 'il ballo de torchio' which was still used to end a banquet when he was writing about 1530, and Shakespeare's direct source, Arthur Brooke, describes how 'with torch in hand a comely knight did fetch [Juliet] forth to dance'.[6] In the play, Juliet *is* dancing with a knight when Romeo says that 'she doth teach the torches to burn bright' (I. v. 42), so it can be concluded that Shakespeare's dancers are in fact meant to hold torches. The movement of these *flambeaux* is a visual presentation of the light which, figuratively, illumines so many great moments in the play. And it is part of the dance in which Romeo and Juliet do not participate together. The pattern of their love is not to be the harmonious regularity of these man-made stars, the torches, or the dancers themselves, those 'Earth-treading stars that make dark heaven light' as Juliet's father calls them (I. ii. 25); already, at the ball, this harmony is being counterpointed by Tybalt's angry outburst to old Capulet.

The next dancing image in the play is in Mercutio's challenge to Tybalt: 'An thou make minstrels of us, look to hear nothing but discords. Here's my fiddlestick; here's that shall make you dance' (III. i. 44–6). The choreography of the swordplay, and its result, runs counter to the harmony of the dance but the scene has other ironic parallels with the ball. In both, Romeo is to begin with a bystander, not a participant. At the ball, the measure done, there is a declaration of newborn love; in the street, the fighting finished, there is a death. To Juliet, Romeo kissed 'by th' book' (I. v. 108); to Mercutio, Tybalt 'fights by the book of arithmetic' (III. i. 98).

After this first death there are no more images of dancing in the play, and this is consistent with Shakespeare's use of dance imagery elsewhere. The flaring torch, however, linked by Romeo with Juliet's beauty, and a part of the dance itself, occurs briefly as an image in their farewell (III. v. 14), and is physically an essential part of the final scene. At the banquet the torches moved in harmonious concord; in the graveyard, Paris extinguishes his torch as he comes to the Capulet vault; Romeo's lights him to his death, and is placed, unmoving, in the tomb. The stars, no longer surrounding images for love, are now inauspicious, and a yoke on Romeo's 'world-wearied flesh' (v. iii. 112). The dislocation of life is reflected in this dramatic use of the torch, which has a direct, ironic, relation with the *ballo* of the first act.

Dance, then, adds to the play's pervading ironic structure. It is also a physical presentation of a major theme of imagery in the play, and it is a visual comment on the star-crossed universe of the lovers.

There is no dancing in *Hamlet*, though there are a couple of references. Hamlet's pejorative use of 'jig' at II. ii. 494 has already been noticed in Chapter 1, and there is his tantalising quotation of the epitaph for the hobby-horse of the morris dance, 'For O, for O, the hobby-horse is forgot' (III. ii. 129).[7] Othello mentions dancing twice, the first time as part of the celebrations he orders on Cyprus on his wedding night, the second time among a list of Desdemona's accomplishments. The gigantic tortured world of *King Lear* contains nothing of the dance, and when Shakespeare at last uses it in his mature tragedy he places it in the supernatural realm.

The weird sisters in *Macbeth* may be fairies, they may be some other kind of supernatural beings, they may be humans possessed of the devil.[8] The word 'witch' occurs only twice in the play's dialogue, at I. iii. 6 and IV. i. 23, and only the first of these, ' "Aroint thee, witch!" the rump-fed ronyon cries', refers to any of the weird sisters. Their species may be uncertain, their evil is beyond doubt. As the fairies dance at the end of *A Midsummer Night's Dream* to ensure harmony and bring blessings, the witches dance near the beginning of *Macbeth* to foster deceit and destruction:

> The Weird Sisters, hand in hand,
> Posters of the sea and land,
> Thus do go about, about;
> Thrice to thine, and thrice to mine,
> And thrice again, to make up nine.
> Peace! The charm's wound up.
>
> (1. iii. 32–7)

Three and its square, nine, are odd numbers with ancient magical and cabbalistic significance, and are frequently used in ritual dance. Apart from being the number of the witches themselves, three occurs several times in the fabric of the play. Macbeth's titles are three – Thane of Glamis, Thane of Cawdor and King. The first murder involves three deaths, Duncan's and the two grooms'. There are three murderers to kill Banquo, curiously enough in Act III Scene iii. Three apparitions appear in IV. i and not unexpectedly there are several other uses of three in this scene of magic. The triad, then, is a recurring element in the play.

One of the more potent triadic images for the Renaissance was formed by the three Graces. With arms entwined, 'daucing an endlesse round',[9] they represented, among many ideas, the triple rhythm of generosity – giving, accepting and returning; they also symbolised love. Christianised, they represented holy love which is given by God to man, who is thus enraptured and then, in a state of ecstasy, returns the love to God, so that an eternal cycle of love and praise is set up.[10] Ficino's application of this idea to love and beauty has already been noticed in relation to *Romeo and Juliet*.

As the Graces represent love and beauty, the witches represent and engender hate and ugliness. They may even be the spirits 'that tend on mortal thoughts', the 'murdering ministers' that Lady Macbeth calls upon in I. v; her chilling speech closely follows on her reading of Macbeth's letter, of which the first words we hear are, 'They met me in the day of success' (I. v. i). That they are ugly is obvious from Banquo's mention of their 'skinny lips' and 'beards' (I. iii. 45–6) and Macbeth's later greeting to them, 'How now, you secret, black, and midnight hags!' (IV. i. 47). Less obvious is their reversal of the Graces in their character as charities, or thanks, which stems from Seneca's words in *De Beneficiis*,

> Why walkes that knot in a roundell hand in hand? It is in this respect, that a good turne passing orderly from hand too hand, dooth neuerthelesse returne too the giuer: and the grace of the whole is mard, if it bee anywhere broken of: but is most beautiful, if it continew toogether and keepe his course.[11]

An additional later moral was found in the position of the Graces, one with her back to us, the others facing us, because two benefits are supposed to return from one given, though not everyone agreed with this interpretation.[12] The idea of giving, accepting and returning with increased value is presented in reverse in the first witch's story of the sailor's wife who munched chestnuts. The witch asked for some, was refused, and therefore plans revenge; the result for the sailor's wife will be sorrow, not ecstasy.

This prefigures events in the play, for the circular motion of giving, accepting and returning is again perverted in the relationship of Duncan and Macbeth, as it is presented in the continuation of the same scene. The cycle begins when Ross and Angus enter to say, 'The King hath happily receiv'd, Macbeth,/The news of thy success' (I. iii. 89–90), and 'We are sent/To give thee, from our royal master, thanks' (ll. 100–1); the thaneship of Cawdor is then bestowed and the triad is complete (l. 105). Macbeth's gift, success in battle, has been received by Duncan, and given back in a more glorious form. The honour, that is the gift which Macbeth receives, should then be transmuted into another, greater benefit to be returned to the giver, the king, and so the continuous movement should go on. Macbeth mars it by murdering Duncan.

The Graces were depicted naked 'because graces must be free of deceit'[13] or, if clothed, then like Botticelli's Graces in the 'Primavera' they wore 'looce garmentes, howbeit very sheere and thin' as Golding translates it.[14] The witches however are explicitly described by Banquo as 'so wild in their attire' (I. iii. 40) and he later calls upon them 'I' th' name of truth' (I. iii. 52) to tell whether they are 'fantastical' or 'outwardly' what they show. They are certainly not free of deceit, since by the equivocal statements made by themselves and by their masters, who appear as apparitions in Act IV, they induce in Macbeth the false security which plays so large a part in his downfall.

The first dance of the witches travesties the ever-circling dance of the Graces and it is undoubtedly Shakespearian. It is a carole, the words being chanted rather than sung. Linking hands, the weird sisters make a circle, moving first to the right, then probably to the left, then to the right again; they would certainly have begun on the right foot, and moved widdershins, that is, in an anticlockwise direction.[15] All normal dances began with the left foot for reasons, now long lost, of sympathetic magic. The witches' is a ritual dance to make a charm, using mystic numbers, and it is completely justified dramatically.

The other dances, in Act IV Scene i, are almost certainly interpolated. The first is danced around the cauldron at Hecate's command, to enchant the foul ingredients of the pot. This dance is superfluous because the witches have already pronounced their charm 'firm and good' (IV. i. 38) before Hecate arrives. The second is performed to cheer up Macbeth after he has seen the apparitions – a rather thin excuse. Moreover, if the earlier entry of Hecate is spurious, there is a fair case for thinking this second dance is also. One of the witches says, 'I'll charm the air to give a sound,/While you perform your antic round' (IV. i. 129–30). If just Shakespeare's witches were on the stage, this would leave only two of them to dance the round. Two would be adequate, but the dance would be far more effective if performed by several. Ben Jonson has given a full description of the kind of grotesque movements that would have been made, in his annotations for *The Masque of Queens*.[16] The Folio stage direction for Hecate's entrance earlier in the scene is: 'Enter Hecate and the other witches'. This has been emended variously to: 'Enter Hecate to the other three witches' or simply: 'Enter Hecate'.[17] It is very likely that the 'other witches' of the stage direction were brought in specially to make up the numbers for more spectacular dancing, first around the cauldron and then in the 'antic round'. Neither of these is essential to the play, both are performed to music, which is not used in the dance of the first act, and both of them hold up the action.

These dances are unique in Shakespeare's plays because they are not dramatically relevant, and this lack of relevance is a further reason, if more are still needed, for considering them spurious. The ritual dance of Act I, however, is important structurally in that it is the preparation of a charm. It travesties the dance as a symbol of harmony and, whether or not intentionally, it is a visual perversion of the dance of the three Graces. Moreover, by emphasising so strongly the triadic image, in the third scene of the first act, the dance contributes importantly to the supernatural element in the play.

In *Antony and Cleopatra* the supernatural is signified by music; when hautboys are played under the stage in Act IV Scene iii one of the soldiers interprets the unearthly sound as an indication that 'the god Hercules, whom Antony lov'd' is leaving him. By this time Antony's decline has gathered the momentum of inevitability, but the disintegration of the triumvirate, and of Antony's world, has already been symbolically presented in Act II Scene vii, in which the triumvirs come to a feast on board Pompey's galley to celebrate the queasy peace that Caesar and Antony have just arranged with him. The substance of the scene is from Plutarch[18] but Shakespeare adds enormous implications to it by showing the rulers of the world drunk and by making an inebriated dance the climax. The meaning of the dance and its accompanying song is in powerful ironic counterpoint to the vast grandeur of the cosmic imagery which gives so much to the tone of the play.

Two servants, commenting on the weakness of great men, particularly the triumvir Lepidus, introduce the scene, and the cosmic theme enters into the last sentence of their exchange when one says, 'To be call'd into a huge sphere, and not to be seen to move in't, are the holes where eyes should be, which pitifully disaster the cheeks' (ii. vii. 13–16), that is, to be one among great men, but to have no influence, is as if a head were bereft of its eyes. A gruesome comparison, setting the mood for a scene which begins with talk of mud, slime, serpents and crocodiles, and Antony's making fun of Lepidus, and moves through Menas's suggestion to Pompey that the drunken triumvirs could be murdered, leaving Pompey 'lord of the whole world', to the bearing out of the by now insensible Lepidus – the eyes indeed sightless. Pompey rejects Menas's plan, though he says that he would have 'found it afterward well done' if Menas had carried out the assassinations without telling him first.

It is Enobarbus, acting as a master of ceremonies, who suggests the dance:

> Ha, my brave emperor!
> Shall we dance now the Egyptian Bacchanals
> And celebrate our drink?
>
> (ii. vii. 102–4)

He commands that everyone shall sing the chorus of the song to Bacchus, then joins them hand in hand. The refrain, 'Cup us till the world go round' refers in its immediate context to the dizziness affecting the drinkers but it is also a deeper comment on the disorder underlying the revelry, during which the word 'world' is used five times in less than a hundred lines. One of the servants considers that some of the revellers are already like ill-rooted plants, 'the least wind i' th' world will blow them down' (l. 3), and it is clear from his conversation that there is still some friction among the three leaders;[19] Menas offers Pompey the world, through treachery; the triumvirs are termed 'world-sharers' (l. 69); and Enobarbus points out to Menas that the servant carrying off the comatose Lepidus is a strong fellow, since he 'bears the third part of the world' (l. 88). This ignominious departure is a visual indication of the breaking-up of the triumvirate; Lepidus does not take part in the dance and he does not appear again in the play. Dancing, which should represent harmony and order by the regular pattern of its movement, in *Antony and Cleopatra* is in drunken disarray, and it prefigures the greater disorder which follows.

In Act i Scene ii of *Timon of Athens* Shakespeare introduces for the first time in his plays dancing by characters who have no other part in the dramatic action. The occasion is Timon's masque to entertain his guests, and it begins in a way typical of certain kinds of masques since Henry VII's time, with a noise outside the banqueting hall heralding the unexpected arrival of newcomers. The host expresses surprise, then a messenger enters to announce the purpose of the visit and present the entertainment: in this case Cupid ushers in 'a Masque of Ladies as Amazons, with lutes in their hands, dancing and playing'. When the ladies have performed, Timon's guests 'rise from table, with much adoring of Timon; and to show their loves, each single out an Amazon, and all dance, men with women, a lofty strain or two to the hautboys, and cease'. In thanking them Timon says they have entertained him with his 'own device' and invites them to partake of 'an idle banquet'; the ladies and Cupid accept the invitation and go out of the room, and out of the play.

Why should Shakespeare's Timon entertain his guests with a masque? Why a masque of Amazons? None of the play's sources or analogues contains a similar event.

For over a century masquing had been a favourite royal diversion, but the English court masque had entered its most glorious period with James's ascent to the throne in 1603. One of the most notable of the early masques was given at the wedding celebrations of Sir Philip Herbert and Lady Susan Vere on St John's Day, 27 December 1604. The fortunately garrulous John Chamberlain wrote to Sir Ralph Winwood on 18 December,

> Here is a great provision of masks and revells against the marriage of Sir Phillip Herbert and Lady Susan Vere, which is to be celebrated on St. John's Day; The Queen hath likewise a great mask in hand against Twelfth-tide, for which there was 3000 l. delivered a month ago.[20]

Queen Anne's 'great mask' was Ben Jonson's first for the court, *The Masque of Blackness*. This was followed in January 1606 by his *Hymenaei*, for the unfortunate marriage of Frances Howard and Robert Earl of Essex, and in July of the same year by an entertainment at Theobalds for the Danish King Christian IV's visit, during which the drunkenness of the kings and courtiers, ladies and gentlemen, disgraced both nations.[21] Campion's masque for Lord Hay's marriage was presented at court in January 1606, a year later came Jonson's *Masque of Beauty*, and then his *Hue and Cry After*

*Cupid*, for the marriage of Viscount Haddington. As it is to some time during these years, 1604–8, that *Timon of Athens* is usually assigned,[22] Shakespeare's inclusion of the masque is consonant with the success of this form of entertainment at court.

There are no Amazons in any extant English masques contemporary with *Timon*, although there had been a *Mask of Amazons* at Queen Elizabeth's court during the Christmas celebrations of 1579. In France royal masquers had appeared as Amazons in 1565 and 1572,[23] but in the English court there were no more Amazons until Jonson's *Masque of Queens* in February 1609, when Lucy, Countess of Bedford, appeared as Penthesilea, the Amazon leader. In his notes to the text, Jonson says that Penthesilea 'is no where mentioned, but with the præface of Honor, and virtue; and is allwayes aduancd in the head, of the worthiest women'[24] but elsewhere he is less complimentary about the warrior queen. *Epicoene's* Morose bitterly discovering his new wife's loquacity, cries, 'She is my regent already! I have married a Penthesilea, a Semiramis, sold my liberty to a distaffe!' (III. iv. 51–2). He later speaks of her 'Amazonian impudence!' (III. v. 39), while in the final speech of the play Truewit cocks an ironic eye at the 'heroine's' revelation as a boy, calling her 'this Amazon, the champion of the sex' (v. iv. 212).

The generally accepted use of 'Amazon' of the period was this latter, which presented the Amazon as the type of the unfeminine woman. When Spenser's Radigund (*The Faerie Queene*, v, iv–vii) captures Artegall, she forces him to dress as a woman and do menial tasks – her usual practice with male conquests. Uncharacteristically, she falls in love with Artegall but he is saved by the arrival of Britomart, who decapitates his unfortunate gaoler. Although she wields arms so effectively, Britomart remains truly feminine, and it is only the villainous and unnatural Radigund who is an Amazon. The most ambiguous Amazon must be Sidney's Pyrocles, who disguises himself as Zelmane so that he can pursue his love for Philoclea; this results in her father, Basilius, falling into 'such a doting love' with him/her that Pyrocles is 'even choaked with his tediousness', but it also leads to Philoclea's mother, Gynecia, 'a woman of excellent witte, and of strong working thoughts', seeing through the disguise and falling in love with the man beneath, as indeed Philoclea does also.[25]

Whenever Shakespeare refers to Amazons it is to emphasise their warlike quality and to contrast them with womanly women. The scornful Titania ridicules Hyppolyta as 'the bouncing Amazon' (*A*

*Midsummer Night's Dream* II. i. 70), and the Bastard in *King John* describes how 'ladies and pale-visag'd maids,/Like Amazons . . ./ Their thimbles into armed gauntlets change,/ . . . and their gentle hearts/To fierce and bloody inclination' (v. ii. 154–8). When the Pucelle defeats the Dauphin in single combat he cries, 'Stay, stay thy hands; thou art an Amazon' (*1 Henry VI*, I. ii. 104) and on being told that Queen Margaret is 'ready to put armour on', King Edward says, 'Belike she minds to play the Amazon' (*3 Henry VI*, IV. i. 106). This echoes an earlier cry by York, as Margaret leads his torment before he is murdered,

> How ill-beseeming is it in thy sex
> To triumph like an Amazonian trull
> Upon their woes whom fortune captivates!
> 
> (*3 Henry VI*, I. iv. 113–15)

The added sexual implication of 'trull' is also found in Rabelais. Describing the army led by Loupgarou, Panurge's prisoner tells him it contains, as well as foot soldiers, cuirassiers, cannons, harquebusiers and pioneers, 'one hundred and fifty thousand whores, fair like goddesses, (that is for me, said Panurge,) whereof some are Amazons, some Lionnoises, others Parisiennes, Tourangelles, Angevines, Poichevines, Normands, and High Dutch – there are of them all countries and all languages'.[26] On the masquing stage Amazons may have been theatrically colourful, but their connotations were negative – belligerent, unfeminine and destructive.

The only women in *Timon of Athens* apart from the dancers in the masque are the whores, significantly named Phrynia and Timandra. Phryne was a Greek courtesan of extraordinary beauty, who, it is said, modelled for Apelles' celebrated picture, 'Venus Anadyomene', and in North's Plutarch, Timandra was the name of Alcibiades' concubine who buried him honourably after his murder. When Shakespeare's Alcibiades approaches Timon with the two whores, in Act IV of the play, they are announced by a drum and fife, as the Amazons in the masque were announced by a trumpet. Timon tells him to paint the ground with men's blood, in battle, and continues,

> This fell whore of thine
> Hath in her more destruction than thy sword
> For all her cherubin look.
> 
> (IV. iii. 60–2)

These words and the presence of the whores themselves form an explicit statement of the images of depravity and destruction evoked in the first act by the masque of Amazons and by the grim philosophising of Apemantus to which it gives rise. According to some sources, Amazons destroyed any men who came within their boundaries; the ladies of the masque hide their true nature under the glamour of their beauty. Apemantus's crabbed comments begin with a distinctly puritan flavour:

> Hoy-day, what a sweep of vanity comes this way!
> They dance? They are mad women.
>
> (i. ii. 126–7)

And finishes with a warning so prophetic that it becomes a reference point for the play's action:

> I should fear those that dance before me now
> Would one day stamp upon me. 'T has been done:
> Men shut their doors against a setting sun.
>
> (i. ii. 137–9)

The comment is visually reinforced when, straight after Apemantus has finished, 'The Lords rise from table, with much adoring of Timon' and dance with the ladies. The situation contains much irony. This concluding part of a masque, the taking out of members of the audience by the masquers, represented the fusion of the illusory world of the masque with the real world, the dance symbolising concord between the two. In the world of *Timon of Athens*, this symbol is itself hollow, since it is the cynical words of Apemantus which carry truth for the future, not the harmonious unity of the dance. Dramatically the masque as a whole is an ironic device on the part of Shakespeare, but not Timon. It is a prelude to hatred, but is introduced by Cupid, the god of love, and the Amazons, masculine women, are aberrations in themselves; as warriors they should carry swords, but instead they carry lutes in their hands.[27] Their dancing provides a harmonious background to the sour moralising of Apemantus; and his concluding remarks prefigure the course of the play.

Masquing is the presentation of illusion, and the masque of Amazons is a lively representation of the wealth that Timon imagines he still possesses. Stephen Orgel's remark, 'A test of the importance of the masque as an instrument of royal policy may be found in the large sums of money lavished on such courtly spectacles, even when the crown was heavily in debt',[28] can be applied to Timon as well as to King James I. Like the feasts, the gifts, the other kindnesses he provides through his wealth, the masque is yet another, more spectacular, form of Timon's prodigal bounty and his steward Flavius, trying to make him see the error of his liberality, in anguished mockery calls him 'Great Timon, noble, worthy, royal Timon!' (ii. ii. 169). David Cook sees the masque as an aspect of Timon's pride which symbolically sets him 'above mere mankind who have to war with the human condition',[29] a view with more substance than A. S. Collins' remark that 'amazingly in a Shakespearean play there are no women, for the Mask of Amazons is only a Mask, and Phrynia and Timandra are mere stage properties'.[30] Rather than being 'mere stage properties', the whores of Act iv have a strong thematic link with the Amazons of Act i, and the dancing is an ironic visual symbol of the perversity which Timon discovers in mankind.

The dance in Shakespeare's tragedies always occurs in the first half of the plays, never at the end, and in each of them it makes a dramatically relevant comment on the action to follow. It is, in fact, part of the Shakespearian arsenal of dramatic irony, for the usual meaning of dance as harmonious amity is posed against the disorder which develops during the course of tragedy. The pattern, established in *Romeo and Juliet*, is elaborated in *Macbeth* by the occult significance of the number three; in *Antony and Cleopatra* a drunken dance is a nexus of plot and relationships and a symbol for a falling world, and in *Timon of Athens* a masque of Amazons reflects on the hero's present generosity and his future disenchantment.

# 6 The Last Plays I

As in a Quire of well tun'd voyced Men,
    When the first man hath giu'n the first accent,
    There doth ensue a noise melodious then
    Of all the voyces, ioyn'd in one consent:
    So God by powre, super-omnivalent,
    Giuing first motion, to the highest Sphere,
    (Being first Mouer) then incontinent,
    All lower Bodies orderly did steere,
As by their present motion doth appeare.
        John Davies of Hereford, *Mirum in Modum* (1602),
                        sig. H2v.

In the final plays dancing is once again associated with harmony as it had been in the comedies but it is now also related to discord, for these plays are a culmination, gathering into themselves many of the ideas, methods and devices of all that Shakespeare had written before. By this connection with both concord and disorder the dance contributes to the distinctive tone of the plays, in which the apparently tragic is transmuted into a state that, while not always of serene and utter joy, nevertheless holds optimistic promise for the future. In *Pericles, Cymbeline, The Winter's Tale* and *The Tempest* this change is brought about particularly through the boundless conventions of romance; in *Henry VIII* history is translated on to the stage with similar effect. Each of the plays contains a strong religious element, all five are ceremonial to a degree and ritual reaches its climax in *Henry VIII*.

In addition to the reasons suggested at the end of Chapter 1 for the inclusion of dances and shows in these plays, sound circumstantial evidence for the direct influence of the attitude of the court, particularly of King James, comes from *The Two Noble Kinsmen*, now generally accepted as being written by Shakespeare and Fletcher in 1613. The entertainment in III. v of that play is composed of characters and dances from the second antimasque of

Francis Beaumont's *Masque of the Inner Temple and Gray's Inn*, given at Whitehall on 20 February 1613 as part of the wedding celebrations of the Princess Elizabeth and the Elector Palatine. When the masque was finally presented, after its initial postponement, this antimasque so pleased the King that he called for it to be repeated when the whole performance ended. It seems probable that such royal approval may have led the authors to ask Fletcher's former collaborator to allow them to include it in their play. An earlier instance is provided by *Macbeth*, in which the dancing of the witches in I. iii and show of kings in IV. i., so complimentary to James, can be attributed in part if not wholly to the sovereign's known interest in the supernatural and in theatrical spectacle. The dance, music, song, costume and staging which make up that spectacle in the last plays add fundamentally to their meaning, however they are conceived – as myths of regeneration, expositions of forgiveness, expressions of nationalism or, at their simplest, what they basically are, tales of wonder and delight.[1]

The first of the group was *Pericles*, parts of which may not be by Shakespeare, but which was being acted at the Globe by the King's Men in 1608, the year the company leased the Blackfriars theatre.[2] Whether or not Shakespeare was responsible for the play's overall conception and structure but for only some of its composition, dance is used in familiarly Shakespearian ways, as a function of plot and characterisation and as matter for imagery. When Pericles, in the first scene, guesses the riddle that would win him the beautiful daughter of Antiochus he is horrified at discovering that the answer reveals an incestuous union between the princess and her father; in an aside resounding with cosmic implications he says of her,

> You are a fair viol, and your sense the strings;
> Who, finger'd to make man his lawful music,
> Would draw heaven down, and all the gods, to hearken;
> But, being play'd upon before your time,
> Hell only danceth at so harsh a chime.
>
> (I. i. 81–5)

This, the play's first image of dance, pictures monstrous disharmony, pointedly opposing music's affinity with heaven and the whole frame of order to the discord of hell. It strongly recalls an illustration of the monochord of the universe in Robert Fludd's *Utriusque cosmi majoris scilicet et minoris metaphysica, physica atque technica historia* (1617–19) which shows a monochord, a single-stringed instrument, which reaches from the lowest to the highest in the universe with God's hand stretching out from a cloud to tune it.[3] The incest of the king of Antioch and his daughter, seen by Pericles to be as the chaos of hell, represents evil in government, the destruction of family life and the corruption of individuals. It has caused the deaths of all the previous suitors to the princess, whose skulls look down on Pericles, and would lead to his as well were he not to escape. Through further tribulation the play progresses to final harmony – of single souls, particularly the hero's, of families, in the reunion of Pericles, Thaisa and their child, Marina, and, although it is not stressed, of the state, in the restoration of health to a diseased city, Mytilene, through the conversion of its governor, Lysimachus, and his marriage to Marina. On four occasions dance has a part in this movement towards resolution.

In Act II Pericles survives the first of the play's tempests at sea, to be cast on the shores of Pentapolis. There, the fishermen's miraculous draft of his armour enables him to compete in a tourney for the love of Thaisa, the daughter of King Simonides. Just before he had answered the riddle of Antiochus, Pericles had compared himself to a knight in a tournament:

> Like a bold champion I assume the lists,
> Nor ask advice of any other thought
> But faithfulness and courage.
>
> (I. i. 61–3)

Now he becomes the champion who both assumes the lists and wins the lady – and this time the lady is worth the winning. The tournament, which takes place off the stage, is preceded by a parade of six knights, each except the last with a squire who presents to Thaisa a shield emblazoned with an impresa – an emblematic device and motto. The last knight is, of course, Pericles, who has to deliver up his shield himself, which he does with 'graceful courtesy'. In early productions, this parade of knights would probably have been a high point of the play's spectacle, the knights in armour, with plumed helmets, their decorated shields proudly borne by the squires. Neither this pageantry nor the tournament itself, which as well as being offstage is quickly over, is found in the two main sources for the play, Book 8 of the *Confessio Amantis* of John Gower, 'this worthy olde writer' as the preface to the 1554 edition calls him, and *The Patterne of Painefull Aduentures* (1576), Laurence Twine's translation of a French version of the 153rd story from the *Gesta Romanorum*. Instead Gower has an athletics contest and Twine a far less impressive tennis match. Such parades of knights and pages with impresa shields were not unknown on the stage,[4] plays in which they had been seen including Kyd's *Spanish Tragedy* (*c*. 1582–92) and *Soliman and Perseda* (*c*. 1590) but more strikingly Middleton's *Your Five Gallants*, (*c*. 1604–7), in which the eponymous gallants are five villains who are seeking the hand of Katherine, a wealthy orphan. In the last act they present themselves to her in a masque as knights, each preceded by a boy holding an emblazoned shield. The mottoes have been devised by the play's hero, Fitsgrave, so that they are ambiguous and can be interpreted as good by the suitors while in reality describing their particular vices, thus abetting their exposure. The spectacle is closely woven into the texture of the play, which was written within a few years of *Pericles* and performed by a boys' company under Robert Keysar at the Blackfriars. Considering the rivalry at this time between the boys' companies and the men's, particularly the King's Men, it is to be wondered if this pageantry in *Pericles* was a deliberate attempt to outshine the masque in Middleton's play. A broader reason for the inclusion of such scenes in both plays may well lie in the increasing popularity of tournaments as court entertainments.

The presentation of these tournaments, as revivals of medieval chivalry, is well documented.[5] Queen Elizabeth's Accession Day, 17 November, had been the occasion for tilts, as they were called, organised by Sir Henry Lee, the Queen's Champion until he retired in 1590. The glamorous splendour of these displays, which evoked chivalric feelings to surround a virgin queen, were also used to dazzle foreign visitors; during Elizabeth's reign, for example, tilts were staged in April, May and June 1581 for the commissioners for the proposed marriage with Alençon. When James came to the throne he transferred the tilts to his own Accession Day, 24 March, and they were also held on other celebratory occasions, which rapidly increased in number after 1603; in 1605, for instance, as well as the Accession Day tilt there were similar entertainments on 4 and 9 April and 20 May; on 5 August 1606 a tilt was part of the lavish entertainment for Christian IV of Denmark and on 25 May 1607 there was another for the visiting Prince Joinville. It is not too fanciful to suggest that the chivalric shows of *Your Five Gallants* and *Pericles* are a reflection of these royal displays.

The magnificence of plumed helmets and knightly costumes of the court tournaments and masques can, happily, still be realised from the designs of Inigo Jones, the accounts of the Revels office with their lists of items for which payments had to be made, and descriptions like Ben Jonson's from his text for the Barriers at Whitehall on Twelfth Night 1606 as part of the celebration for the Essex marriage. (For the Barriers, an indoor combat on foot, a bar was set up and the knights addressed themselves for fight on either side.)

> At the lower end of the hall a march being sounded with drummes and phifes, there entred (led foorth by the Earle of Nottingham, who was lord high Constable for that night, and the Earle of Worc'ster, Earle Marshall) sixteene knights, armed with pikes, and swords; their plumes, and colours, carnation and white, all richly accoutred; and making their honors to the state, as they march'd by in paires, were all rank'd on one side of the hall. They plac'd, sixteene others like accoutred for riches, and armes, only that their colours were varied to watchet, and white; were by the same Earles led vp, and passing in like manner, by the state, plac'd on the opposite side.
>
> (ll. 849–60)

Even if such extravagance were beyond the normal resources of a theatrical company, the allegorical significance of heraldic devices could be, and was, used dramatically. In *Your Five Gallants* Middleton integrates the ceremonial and his plot with a sophisticated irony that looks forward to the chess game of his *Women Beware Women* (*c.* 1621). The value of the parade in *Pericles* lies mainly in its spectacle, but it also forwards the story by introducing the hero in a 'dejected state', with rusty armour and no squire. Being unattended, Pericles must present his shield himself so that he comes face to face with the Princess Thaisa and also arouses a favourable comment from her father. The tournament allows him to distinguish himself as an heroic figure when he wins the combat. Despite his victory, Pericles is a moody guest at the ensuing banquet and to 'awaken him from his melancholy' Simonides calls for a dance by the knights:

> Even in your armours, as you are address'd,
> Will very well become a solder's dance.
>
> (II. iii. 95–6)

This done, the King encourages Pericles to dance with his daughter, making at least one and possibly two puns as he does so:

> Come, sir;
> Here is a lady that wants breathing [i.e. exercising] too;
> And I have heard you knights of Tyre
> Are excellent in making ladies trip;
> And that their measures are as excellent.
> *Pericles*  In those that practise them they are, my lord.

(II. iii. 100–5)

The first dance may be for both men and women, for the text is ambiguous, but it would be more appropriate for the knights to dance alone, perhaps presenting a mock battle by dancing the matachin in armour. Harington writes in *The Metamorphosis of Ajax* (1596) of having seen 'Matachinas' as part of stage plays; in the *Arcadia* I. 17 (1590) Sidney mentions a matachin dance which imitated fighting and on Twelfth Night 1605 there was a play at court 'with a masquerade of certaine Scotchmen who come in with a sword dance not unlike a matachin'; Arbeau describes one version in *Orchesography*, linking it with the pyrrhic dance of classical times.[6] The clash of arms in this kind of dance seems to be implied when Simonides says (with another pun in the last line),

> Even in your armours, as you are address'd,
> Will very well become a solder's dance.
> I will not have excuse, with saying this
> Loud music is too harsh for ladies' heads,
> Since they love men in arms as well as beds.

(II. iii. 95–9)

Certainly the knights dance with the ladies after this, and they are thanked by their host, who singles out Pericles for special praise,

> Thanks, gentlemen, to all; all have done well,
> [*To Pericles*] But you the best.

(108–9)

The play follows its main sources in the presentation of the banquet, but where in Gower the hero, Apollonius,

> tak'th the harpe, and in his wise
> He tempreth, and of such assaise
> Synginge he harpeth forth with all,[7]

and in Twine the hero plays the harp 'with such cunning and sweetness, that he seemed rather to be Apollo than Apollonius'[8], George Wilkins' *Painfull Aduentures of Pericles Prince of Tyre*, which claims to be 'the True history of the play of Pericles', omits specific mention of Pericles' playing or dancing; it concludes the account of the banquet with, 'Much time being spent in dancing and other reuells, the night being growne olde, the King commanded the Knights should be conducted to their lodgings'.[9] This change from singing to dancing is at one with the change from Gower's athletics contest and Twine's tennis match to the parade of knights and the tourney which follows. All are more theatrical, they have more potential for symbolism, they are more visual and they are more topical.

As in the tragedies, the dancing in *Pericles* occurs in the first half of the play, which then moves towards tragedy; but the idea of dance, if not the physical action, is present in the later parts, especially in relation to Marina. During the storm which is the play's pivotal centre, the apparently destructive storm in which Thaisa 'dies' and Marina is born, Pericles prays,

> Lucina, O
> Divinest patroness, and midwife gentle
> To those that cry by night, convey thy deity
> Aboard our dancing boat; make swift the pangs
> Of my queen's travails!
>
> (III. i. 10–14)

Here 'dancing' is a simple descriptive word for the motion of the boat on the storm-racked sea but it has deeper implications for the Pythagorean ideas of the dance of love which brought harmony out of the first chaos of matter. When the nurse, Lychorida, brings the newborn Marina to Pericles – 'all that is left living of your queen' – he takes the child and, in a plea for future harmony, he speaks of the elements,

> Now mild may be thy life!
> . . . . Happy what follows!

Thou hast as chiding a nativity
As fire, air, water, earth, and heaven can make,
To herald thee from the womb.

(27, 31–4)

John Davies of Hereford follows the stanza from *Mirum in Modum*
which provides the epigraph for this chapter with

> Looke on the World, and what it doth comprize,
>    And Sence shall see, all mouing vnto one,
>    The Elementes, and ten-fold orbed Skies,
>    In motion diuerse tend to one alone,
>    And make one World, through their coniunction;
>    The Sea ingirts the Earth; Th'Aire boundeth both,
>    Being compas'd with the Firy region,
>    The Coape of Heau'n, doth seeme them all to cloth,
> Who arme in arme vnto an Vnion goth.

And in the verses for the Barriers at the Essex wedding Jonson writes
of 'Eternall Vnitie . . That fire, and water, earth and ayre com-
bines' (ll. 907–8).

By drawing on this commonplace of cosmology, the verse
surrounding the birth of Marina and the 'death' of Thaisa has
strong associations with the coming of order out of chaos. The
'dancing' boat is a fit cradle for the newborn child who brings
healing goodness into the corrupt world of Mytilene when she
brings divinity to the brothel and converts its clients, who include
the governor of the town, Lysimachus. Later still, she restores
harmony of mind and spirit to her own father. Like the young
Pericles, Marina is 'train'd/in music, letters' (iv. Prol.) and she
escapes from the brothel by bribing the servant, Boult, to proclaim
throughout the town that she can 'sing, weave, sew, and dance,/
With other virtues' (iv. vi. 181–2) which she will undertake to
teach. In his prologue to Act v Gower says that Marina 'sings like
one immortal, and she dances/As goddess-like to her admired lays'
and when Pericles comes to Mytilene mute, deaf and unkempt from
his wandering shipboard vigil, Lysimachus agrees with one of the
lords that

> She, questionless, with her sweet harmony
> And other chosen attractions, would allure,

And make a batt'ry through his deafen'd parts,
Which now are midway stopp'd.

(v. i. 43–7)

Marina's 'chosen attractions' are combined in the great and moving
scene of her reunion with her father, where her singing first awakes
him, her story reassures him and their embrace evokes the music of
the spheres by the heavenly bodies' moving harmoniously around
the earth in the never-ending dance of the cosmos. Pericles danced
'best of all' when he won Thaisa for a bride, Marina was born on a
'dancing boat', she grows to a maiden who dances 'goddess-like'
and now the whole universe dances as they are reunited.

The only play in this study which does not have an explicit
direction for dance is *Cymbeline* but it is included because the vision
of Posthumus in v. iv gives potent expression to many of the play's
themes and images through words, music and visually striking
action which includes ordered movement if not dance itself. When
Posthumus is thrust into his prison cell in chains the first gaoler tells
him,

You shall not now be stol'n, you have locks upon you;
So graze as you find pasture.

(v. iv. 1–2)

In his soliloquy which follows, Posthumus welcomes his bondage
and the cure that the 'sure physician death' can bring and beseeches
the gods to take his life for Imogen's, whom he believes dead: ' 'Tis
not so dear, yet 'tis a life; you coin'd it' (v. iv. 23); and before lying
down to sleep, with his wife's name on his lips, he again begs the
gods to take his life and 'cancel these cold bonds'. The gaoler's
image of an earthbound animal feeding gains strength by its
contrast to the bird imagery which enriches the play in so many
ways and which is first used when Imogen refers to Posthumus as an
eagle (i. i. 139); death pictured as a physician is part of the medical
imagery found especially in this play and *The Winter's Tale*, and the
idea of money is particularly important in *Cymbeline* owing to the
wager between Posthumus and Iachimo over Imogen's chastity.
The wager plot itself is perhaps shadowed as an element of serious
punning in the word 'bonds'.

These reminders of image, theme and plot in the speech of the
hero at the nadir of his fortunes are a prelude to the play's great
spectacle, the apparition of the four Leonati, Posthumus's family,

whose prayer asking Jupiter to have mercy on the prisoner and 'Take off his miseries' is answered by the appearance of the thunderer himself. The stage direction is detailed:

> Solemn Music. Enter, as in an apparition, Sicilius Leonatus, father to Posthumus, an old man attired like a warrior; leading in his hand an ancient matron, his Wife, and mother to Posthumus, with music before them. Then, after other music, follows the two young Leonati, brothers to Posthumus, with wounds, as they died in the wars. They circle Posthumus round as he lies sleeping.
>
> (v. iv. 29. 1–9)

Solemn music, 'the best comforter/To an unsettled fancy' as Prospero calls it in *The Tempest*, is both heard and seen to be played as the two pairs of ghosts are each preceded by musicians; Sicilius, the father, leads his wife by the hand and all the ghosts move around Posthumus in a circle. There are, then, three symbols of harmony: the music itself, the married couple hand in hand and the circle – 'The perfect'st figure is the round', as Jonson says in *Hymenaei* (l. 404). As they move, they sing or rhythmically chant their appeal, which begins with a reminiscence of *King Lear* which also reflects the airborne and avian images of the play:[10]

> *Sici.*   No more, thou thunder-master, show
>    Thy spite on mortal flies.

Even though there is no specific direction that the ghosts dance around the sleeping prisoner it is clearly apparent that they circle him with regular motion, first, because of the music, then because of the pronounced rhythms of the prayer. In social life at the time pavan steps were used in solemn processions, and the masque qualities of the vision, its ritualised form, demand regular movement. The appearance of deities on the masque stage was usually preceded by dancing since the theophany signified, as it does in *Cymbeline*, the introduction of order.[11] An idea of Jupiter's descent in glory may be gained from Inigo Jones's sketch for a similar arrival in Townsend's *Tempe Restored* presented on 14 February 1632 (*Cymbeline* was acted at court on New Year's night 1634. It was 'Well likte by the kinge'.)[12] More relevant, perhaps, is a picture from Giulio Parigi's *Il Giudizio di Paride* (Florence, 1608) which shows Jupiter on an eagle, clutching his thunderbolts and surrounded by his gods and goddesses.[13] The closeness in date of this picture and the play raises the tantalising thought, and it can be no more, that the idea for the play's theophany was like the Roman eagle which the soothsayer in the last scene says came 'on wing soaring aloft' from Italy.

The vision scene in *Cymbeline* occurs at the point in the play where the potential for tragedy is at its greatest and it is the matter at the heart of the spectacle which changes the direction of the action away from disaster to happiness. In this it strongly resembles the moment in a masque when the masquers appear or are revealed, replacing the disorder of the antimasque. (Among Jonson's masques which provide examples are *Queens, Mercury Vindicated, Pleasure Reconciled with Virtue, Pan's Anniversary* and *Chloridia.*) The return to harmony in the last scene, in which the soothsayer who deciphers Jupiter's prophecy is called 'Philarmonus', this resolution into comedy after the most bizarre and complicated plotwork in all Shakespeare, is foreshadowed by the music, by the ordered movement of the spirits of Posthumus's family and by the shape of the circle in which they process. Future concord is assured when Jupiter, in admonitory but benevolent mood, descends on his eagle to answer their prayer and leave the tablet with its riddling prophecy.

Dance is more strongly associated with disharmony in *The Winter's Tale*, where the word itself is first mentioned in a context of jealous rage and murderous hate. At Leontes' urging, the heavily pregnant Hermione has just persuaded Polixenes to stay longer at the Sicilian court. The Bohemian king has been there nine months, and even though he is most anxious to return home, Hermione charms him into staying another week. Leontes praises her:

> thou never spok'st
> To better purpose.
>
> *Her.*                              Never?
> *Leon.*                                    Never but once.
>                      . . . . . that was when
> Three crabbed months had sour'd themselves to
>                                                          death,
> Ere I could make thee open thy white hand
> And clap thyself my love; then didst thou utter
> 'I am yours for ever'.
>
>                                              (I. ii. 88 . . . 105)

It is after this apparently loving and lighthearted exchange that Leontes' furious suspicion, too long repressed, bursts out in the contorted language of

> Too hot, too hot!
> To mingle friendship far is mingling bloods.
> I have tremor cordis on me; my heart dances,
> But not for joy, not joy.
>
> (108–11)

A heart that is dancing, 'but not for joy', implies a savage lack of harmony at the centre of existence. The disorder, moreover, has spread through Leontes' body – 'tremor cordis' is an uncontrollable shaking or trembling due to powerful emotional upset – and it extends through his court and out into the universe.

The cosmic setting for the play has been introduced in the first scene by Camillo when telling Archidamus of the great friendship between Leontes and Polixenes: 'Sicilia cannot show himself overkind to Bohemia . . . The heavens continue their loves!'. To which Archidamus replies, 'I think there is not in the world either malice or matter to alter it'. The idea is developed throughout the next scene, beginning with the first line, in which Polixenes calls the moon 'the wat'ry star' (I. ii. I), and continuing with the characters' use of words like 'world' (20), 'unsphere' (47), 'stars' (47, 425), 'sun' (67), 'Heaven' (73, 315, 425), 'welkin' (136), 'planet' (201) and phrases such as Leontes' 'heaven sees earth and earth sees heaven' (315) and Camillo's little prayer, 'Happy star reign now!' (363). In this connection, Hermione's words to Polixenes when she is trying to persuade him to stay have especial power and significance:

> You put me off with limber vows; but I,
> Though you would seek t'unsphere the stars with oaths,
> Should yet say 'Sir, no going'.
>
> (47–9)

Lightly spoken, the image nevertheless has immense implications, for it is Hermione's successful persuasion of her husband's friend to remain which leads to the dreadful disruption of their lives, and of hers particularly; in terms of the cosmos, unsphering the stars is equivalent to the untuning of the skies, the dislocation of the dance of the heavenly bodies when, as Ulysses says in *Troilus and Cressida*, the planets 'In evil mixture to disorder wander' (I. iii. 95). The image of universal chaos in Hermione's playful banter is in extreme contrast to the intimate internal picture of Leontes' wildly dancing heart but each presages the apparent tragedy of the first part of the play, in which both Leontes and Sicilia lose their harmony. It is a literal and figurative loss, since 'Hermione' was another way of spelling 'Harmonia' (i.e. 'Harmony') during the Renaissance.[14]

The summer warmth of Act IV's Bohemia is more for dancing than Sicilia's grim chilliness and Bohemia itself is a place where dance and song go naturally with celebrations. It is a place where the old shepherd's wife, when she lived,

> welcom'd all; serv'd all;
> Would sing her song and dance her turn,
>
> (IV. iv. 57–8)

and Perdita is expected to do the same. Like Marina, Imogen and Miranda, Perdita has an aura of divinity. Marina 'dances . . . goddess-like', Imogen is 'Cytherea' and for Ferdinand Miranda is the goddess upon whom music attends; the idea is more complicated in *The Winter's Tale* through being introduced by Perdita herself when she self-consciously comments on being a

> poor lowly maid,
> Most goddess-like prank'd up.
>
> (IV. iv. 10)

Her awareness of this role-playing is emphasised later when, having given her flowers and herbs to the disguised Polixenes and Camillo, she turns to her friends and in the most beautiful flower speech in Shakespeare describes the blooms of spring that she wishes she had to bestow on them; but after she has told Florizel with such frank and open charm how she would use the flowers 'To strew him o'er and o'er . . . not to be buried,/But quick, and in mine arms', she checks herself:

> Methinks I play as I have seen them do
> In Whitsun pastorals. Sure, this robe of mine
> Does change my disposition.
>
> (133–5)

As Whitsun was the season of May-games and morris dancing, with
its mock king and its associations with fertility ritual,[15] Perdita's
words gather meaning which illuminates her character even as they
are a preparation for Florizel's reply and the dance of shepherds and
shepherdesses soon after. It is as if recalling the Whitsun May-games
with their attendant licence leads her to think that she has been
indiscreet in what she has just said to her sweetheart; but he
reassures her. Their purity is emphasised when she describes him as
'an unstain'd shepherd' (149) and he tells her that she has 'As little
skill to fear as [he has] purpose' to woo her falsely; he has already
said,

> my desires
> Run not before mine honour, nor my lusts
> Burn hotter than my faith.
>
> (33–5)

Having reaffirmed the chastity of their love, he takes her hand and
leads her in a dance of shepherds and shepherdesses. Appropriately,
this would have been a ring dance, probably a brawl.[16] As has
already been noticed, the English name 'brawl' is a corruption of
'branle', from the French 'branler', meaning to swing from side to
side; the basic steps go alternately from left to right, and there are
many different varieties of the dance, almost all in duple time; two
in triple time are described by Arbeau, who tells us that the branles
are danced sideways, and not stepping forward. They could be
danced in a chain or a circle, with hands linked.[17]

Florizel has already made Perdita's dancing the subject of a
resonant image when he tells her,

> When you do dance, I wish you
> A wave o' the' sea, that you might ever do
> Nothing but that; move still, still so,
> And own no other function.
>
> (140–3)

The sea is a major force in the play, and the phrase 'move still, still
so' contains the idea of movement which remains nevertheless in
one place: a wave rising then slipping back, a dancer swaying to and
fro, back and forth, a ring of dancers moving in a round, circling the
'still point of the turning world'. Now Polixenes comments to the old

shepherd that Perdita 'dances featly'; but a slightly sinister element, at odds with the joyful, ordered dance of the young people and the purity of the lovers, enters with the arrival of Autolycus and the whiff of corruption he brings. He is introduced by the excited, humorously ambiguous announcements of the servant, who says, 'he has the prettiest love-songs for maids, so without bawdry, which is strange; with such delicate burdens of dildos and fadings, "jump her and thump her" . . .' (192–4). As J. H. P. Pafford remarks in the New Arden edition, 'Whatever meanings these burdens may have they are certainly not "delicate" '. He goes on to note that 'Fading' was the name of a jig mentioned in *The Knight of the Burning Pestle* (1607) and that John Playford's *Dancing Master* (1651) contains the round 'Come jump at thy Cosen' with the refrain, 'What jumping, jumping; jumping, jumping call you this'.[18] Here again, as in *Hamlet*, the jig and bawdy are put side by side. The servant's speech modulates the tone of the scene from the innocence of rustic revelry to the crude coarseness of the songs of Autolycus and the disorder covertly introduced with the 'three carters, three shepherds, three neat-herds, three swine-herds, that have made themselves all men of hair [and] call themselves Saltiers' (318–21). Although Warburton suggested that the phrase 'men of hair' was 'taken from tennis-balls, which were stuffed with hair' and so described the nimbleness of the dancers, who 'leap as if they rebounded', and Furness, the Variorum editor, agreed with him, Dr Johnson's gloss, 'hairy men, or satyrs' is surely right, if only because the servant says the dancers have 'made themselves all men of hair'.[19] Pafford comments that 'saltiers' is intended to suggest the dancers' chief attributes: they are good jumpers ('salt', from the French 'sault', was a current word for 'jump') and they are dressed as satyrs.

In the masques and other entertainments of the period in which they appear satyrs are almost invariably associated with disorder, most famously in Jonson's *Oberon, The Fairy Prince*, performed before the King, Queen Anne and Princess Elizabeth on 1 January 1611 with Prince Henry as Oberon, but also in Jonson's *Entertainment at Althorpe* of 1603 and two of James Shirley's masques, *The Triumph of Peace* (1633) and *Cupid and Death* (1651–3). *Oberon* has a particular importance for *The Winter's Tale* because the appearance of satyrs in both (and bears as well, since Oberon's chariot is drawn by two white bears and in the play Antigonus is consumed by a bear) is regarded by many scholars as confirming the play's date at between 1 January and 15 May 1611, when Simon Forman saw it at the

Globe.[20] The theory is attractive and is perhaps supported by the servant's comment that three of the dancers, 'by their own report, sir, hath danc'd before the King' (329). If some of the King's Men had appeared in the antimasque of satyrs in *Oberon* then this statement is just the kind of theatrical joke that would be written into the script for the delectation of the actors themselves; but it also makes a neat ironic point in the world of the play, as the king the dancers are reported to have appeared before is there at the shearing feast, in disguise.

Supposing that some of the King's Men had appeared in the *Oberon* antimasque, it is to be wondered whether the company then hired dancers who had appeared with them as well as sending men to Whitehall for the masque. Since the servant draws attention to their leaping prowess – 'not the worst of the three but jumps twelve foot and a half' (330) – and there are twelve of them, it could be argued that professional tumblers or dancers may have been hired for both masque and play. The scene in *The Winter's Tale* has at least eleven speaking characters, perhaps twelve, and there were probably some others, as shepherds and shepherdesses. It is also the only scene in Shakespeare in which the number of dancers is specified. When the satyrs enter, are at least twenty-three people on the stage. This is a very large number (the final scene of *Cymbeline* manages with twelve speaking parts and two or three others). The implication of the servant's remark that 'one three' of the twelve had danced before the king, then, could be that three of the satyrs were members of the company (£15 for 'Players' was included in the miscellaneous expenses of the masque)[21] and that the other nine were brought in for the play's performance in the theatre.

Alastair Fowler claims that the dance 'is a dance of months or signs, almost in the symbolic manner of *ballets de cour* or masque dances . . . [with] reference to months disposed in their seasons or signs in their humour-governing triplication. Time is now ordered in its parts and ceremonially composed, where earlier it was torn apart'.[22] Time may appear to be seasonally restored by the number of the herdsmen, but their costume and the kind of dance connected with it signify disorder, and twelve is a common number for dancers in antimasques. Twenty-two of Jonson's masques have anti-masques, and ten of these specify twelve performers. Thomas Campion's *Lords' Masque* (1613) also calls for twelve antimasquers.

Whether or not the satyrs and their dance, and the music for it, were borrowed from *Oberon*,[23] their appearance at this point in the play has an important dramatic purpose. In classical mythology the satyrs were lesser divinities connected with the cult of Dionysus, of the same order as the nymphs, centaurs, sileni, Pan and Priapus. They represented the spirits of the woods and forests and by suddenly appearing they would frighten lonely travellers and shepherds. Their horns, goats' legs, tail and cloven hoofs became part of one concept of Satan[24] and although for later mythographers they became gentler of aspect, they are always associated with disorder and licence, particularly sexual licence. They were disturbers of rural peace and symbols of unruled passions. The Italian iconographer Vincenzo Cartari traces a relationship from Jove, 'the first and last of all things', through Pan to the Satyrs. He cites Pausanias who, he says, 'writes of having been told by someone, who was driven by the wind to certain desert islands in the Oceanic sea, called the Satiride, that there lived there wild men, all red, with a tail a little smaller than a horse's, who ran very quickly as soon as they perceived a ship, if there were women aboad, and hurled themselves on them with the greatest fury in the world, molesting them in all possible ways. Which was very likely', Cartari drily adds, 'according to what one reads of Satyrs.' He also refers to Eusebius, who says that Satyrs 'are believed to be libidinous beyond belief'.[25] These attributes provide a strong contrast to the sexual purity and innocence which are so markedly stressed by both Florizel and Perdita and lend weight to the suggestion that the satyrs' dance in the play has emblematic value signifying disorder, in the same way that an antimasque has.

If the satyrs' dance is so considered then the first five hundred lines of Act IV, to the point to where Camillo decides that Florizel and Perdita must go to Sicilia, may be seen as a reverse form of the Jonsonian masque in which, as Stephen Orgel has so amply shown, the disorder expressed by the antimasque of grotesques is dissolved by the appearance of the masquers representing order and benevolence, and the monarch is the symbolic centre from which harmony flows.[26] *Oberon* will serve as well as any, and better than some, as an example of the structure. The opening scene is 'all obscure, & nothing perceiu'd but a darke Rocke, with trees beyond it; and all wildnesse, that could be presented'. A satyr appears and calls up eleven others, who come 'leaping, and making antique action, and gestures'. Their mentor, Silenus, chides them for their rowdy wantonness and expressions of lechery, telling them that Oberon, who 'doth fill with grace/Euery season, eu'ry place', will soon arrive with his knights. The satyrs wake two Sylvans who are guarding the gates of Oberon's palace, then to fill in the time sing an insulting song to the moon, 'yond' seeming maid', and fall 'sodainely into an antique dance, full of gesture, and swift motion'; this is interrupted by the crowing of a cock and Silenus's command, 'Euery Satyre bow his head'. Then, marvellously, the palace opens to discover the fairy kingdom, with 'Oberon, in a chariot, which to a lowd triumphant musique [begins] to moue forward, drawne by two white beares'. The satyrs starting to 'leape and expresse their ioy, for the vn-vsed state, and solemnitie', are reprimanded by the first Sylvan, who explains that Oberon and his court have come to pay homage to King James,

> To whose sole power, and magick they doe giue
> The honor of their being;

Silenus adds,

> Before his presence, you must fall, or flie.

The fairies and elves dance, than after a song 'by all the voyces', Oberon and his knights perform their first masque dance; two more songs and another dance by the masquers are followed by the revels, when they dance 'the measures, coranto's, galliards &c.', until Phosphorus the day star appears and calls them away. After a song by one of the Sylvans the masquers give their last dance and enter their palace, which closes after them.

The basic pattern is of disorder, represented here by the antimasque of the satyrs, resolved by the arrival of order, here in the form of Prince Henry and the courtiers as Oberon and his knights, paying homage to King James, who is thus both part of the masque and yet himself. The songs and dances which follow lead to the revels, in which members of the audience join, and the exit dance of the masquers. Often there was a banquet for masquers and guests after a masque had ended.

In *The Winter's Tale* this pattern is turned on its head. At the beginning of the scene Perdita and Florizel talk of feasting, the old shepherd recalls how his wife had been 'pantler, butler, cook' (56) and Perdita is called 'Mistress o'th' Feast' (68). The love between Perdita and Florizel is wonderfully affirmed, leading to the dance of the shepherds and shepherdesses, equivalent to the masquers'

dance – as indeed it is, since Florizel is disguised as Doricles and
Perdita is wearing the 'borrowed flaunts' of her festival costume, as
well as bearing her unknown identity as Leontes' daughter. This
dance is followed by songs – two by Autolycus, a third by Autolycus,
Mopsa and Dorcas – and the humorous wrangling of the two girls
over the clown's attention. In *Oberon* Jonson prepares the audience
for the resolution of disorder by what Silenus tells the satyrs about
the fairy prince; Shakespeare prepares the way for the approaching
disorder by the trickery of Autolycus and the bawdry of the two
girls. Under a humorous cover, the sinister element is strengthened
by the announcement and arrival of the herdsmen-satyrs, and their
dance, the equivalent of the antimasquers' dance, is followed by
Polixenes' decision to separate the lovers, his doing so, and the
overthrow of order. The satyrs' dance is the culminating preparation for Polixenes' action. During the dance, he has been talking to
the old shepherd – who is 'simple and tells much' (337) – and he
turns to Camillo saying, 'Is it not too far gone? 'Tis time to part them'
(336). During the next eighty lines the tension develops exquisitely
as Florizel and Perdita speak their love and are enjoined by the old
shepherd to 'Take hands, a bargain!', echoing not only Leontes'
reminiscence of his troth-plighting with Hermione (1.ii. 102–4) but
also Hermione's taking Polixenes' hand soon after – the action
which fired Leontes' outburst of jealous rage. Polixenes' insistence
that Florizel's father should know of the betrothal and Florizel's
equally insistent refusal to agree lead to Polixenes' sudden revealing
himself with

> Mark your divorce, young sir,
> Whom son I dare not call; thou art too base
> To be acknowledg'd – thou a sceptre's heir,
> That thus affects a sheep-hook!
>
> (409–12)

The vituperation which follows, aimed at Perdita, is almost as
lunatic as Leontes' ravings had been and it becomes apparent that
the disorder symbolised by the satyr's dance is not just further
intrusion of the court into the countryside, nor the attempted
separation of the lovers – a potentially tragic situation – but the
emotional wildness of Polixenes as well. His passion is extreme: he
breaks a union of true love and he destroys his own family by
disowning Florizel. As the king, he should be the source of order,

instead he is the cause of disruption. The reversed masque pattern is complete when he quits the scene in anger, leaving confusion and dismay in place of harmony and love.[27]

The movement back to order begins quickly, however, with the lovers being organised into going to Sicilia by Camillo, to whom Florizel says, 'It is my father's music/To speak your deeds' (510–11), a phrase pregnant with meaning for the remaining part of the play, for music, rather than dance, becomes the great symbol of harmony in *Pericles*, in *The Winter's Tale* and, especially, in *The Tempest*.

# 7 The Last Plays II

Are they shadowes that we see?
And can shadowes pleasure giue?
Pleasures onely shadowes bee
Cast by bodies we conceiue,
And are made the things we deeme,
In those figures which they seeme.
But these pleasures vanish fast,
Which by shadowes are exprest:
Pleasures are not, if they last,
In their passing, is their best.

Samuel Daniel, *Tethys' Festival* (1610)

Nowhere in Shakespeare is music more important than in *The Tempest*, which of all the plays contains the greatest number of complete songs and the greatest use of atmospheric and dramatically employed music. Like Caliban's island itself the play is 'full of noises,/Sounds, and sweet airs, that give delight, and hurt not' (III. ii. 130). On three occasions the music is related to dance, and on the second and third of these the dancing is also associated with evil. The first time, dance is the subject of a song, the first song in the play, which the invisible Ariel sings to Ferdinand probably in part fulfilment of Prospero's earlier whispered command.

'Come unto these yellow sands' is a magic song, and like much to do with magic, it has ambiguous meaning. It can be seen as a call to the lesser spirits, Ariel's 'quality', to come to the seashore and dance while singing, but it can also be taken as an invitation to the shipwrecked Ferdinand, an allurement enticing him towards Miranda, bidding him to take hands with her, to curtsy, kiss and then dance while the unseen spirits surround them with music. In this way Ariel's singing not only carries the plot onward but foreshadows the harmony of the betrothal and future marriage.

The First Folio text of *The Tempest* is accepted as being exceptionally good, one of the most carefully prepared in the whole volume, but this song provides a textual crux. The Folio version is

> Come vnto these yellow sands,
>     and then take hands:
> Curtsied when you haue, and kist
>     the wilde waues whist:
> Foote it featly heere, and there, and sweete Sprights beare
>                 the burthen.    *Burthen dispersedly.*
> Harke, harke, bowgh wawgh: the watch-Dogges barke,
>                 bowgh-wawgh.
> *Ar.*  Hark, hark, I heare, the straine of strutting Chanticlere
>     cry cockadidle-dowe.

The usually accepted reading follows Warburton's emendation, which would place 'the wild waves whist' in parenthesis, so that the meaning is 'come to the seashore, and when you have curtsied and kissed (the wild waves being silent) then dance'; but this is largely based on the mistaken belief that kissing was a customary part of the beginning of dances. There appears to be no evidence that kissing was a usual part of the honour ('curtsy', 'bow', 'reverence') which preceded a dance, or that a kiss normally came at the end.[1] The syntax of the third and fourth lines would seem clearly to indicate that the kissing has stilled the tempest-tossed waves, so that if the song is taken in the first sense, as a request to the nymphs, it will mean 'Come to the seashore and take hands; when you have curtsied and when you have kissed the waves into silence, then dance and sing the refrain'. Kissing in this transitive sense with a complement is supported by *O.E.D.* (Kiss. v. 4) but the New Arden editor, Frank Kermode, finds the idea 'disagreeable, being grotesque in a context which does not require grotesquerie'. He nevertheless suggests that the syntax should be allowed to be ambiguous, while asserting, 'Of course it was Ariel's music which allayed the tempest' referring to Ferdinand's lines,

> This music crept by me upon the waters,
> Allaying both their fury and my passion
> With its sweet air.
>
>                                 (I. ii. 391–3)

Kissing to calm anger and bring peace is not unusual, however, and since Ariel and, presumably, his nymphs were invisible, Ferdinand would not have seen them at their work but only heard their music. The idea of the nymphs kissing the waves to quieten their tempestuous disorder is not, then, especially grotesque.

It is true that some dances did include embracing as part of a figure. The instructions for 'The Nine Muses', a round dance, include 'honor and embrace' towards the end, for example, and so do those for the 'Madam Sicilla Pavin'; another court dance, the 'Cycyllya Alemayne' has an honour and embrace as two of its figures, one three-quarters the way through and again at the finish.[2] In Heywood's *A Woman Killed with Kindness* (1603) Sisly, a country wench, says meaningly 'I love no dance so well as "John, Come Kiss Me Now" ' (i. ii. 33), naming a round that could be sung with 'Joan' instead of 'John', and in John Playford's book of country dances, *The English Dancing Master* (1651), 'All in a Garden Green', the first in the book's second edition, has the following pleasant directions:

> First man shake his own Woman by the hand, then the 2nd, then the 3rd by one hand, then by the other, kiss her twice and turn her. Shake her by the hand, then the 2nd, then your own by one hand, then by the other; kiss her twice and turn her.[3]

But this is the only example in the collection of 104 dances. That courtly dances sanctioned opportunity for like salutations is clear enough from Henry VIII's remark to Anne Boleyn,

> I were unmannerly to take you out
> And not to kiss you,
>
> (*Henry VIII* i. iv. 95–6)

where 'take you out' means 'dance with you',[4] but this particular kissing is not part of the dance itself, which has ended ten or perhaps twenty lines earlier, and certainly not part of the honour at the beginning.

Anne Righter's note on Ariel's song suggests that 'the ordered measure of the dance stills the sea's violence', but dodges the textual issue by continuing, 'Precisely how this is brought about remains as vague as the syntax'.[5] The syntax is less vague when the comma of the Folio is retained before 'and kissed', so that it is the kissing which stills the waves, rather than the dancing, which follows. The situation may be compared with the reconciliation of Titania and Oberon, after which Oberon says, 'Come, my Queen, take hands with me,/And rock the ground . . . ' (*A Midsummer Night's Dream*, IV. i. 82, and see Chapter 3).

When the song is taken in the second sense, as an invitation to Ferdinand, it is then like the song of the sirens of classical myth in the way it entices; but it is vastly different in that it lures the victim towards good and happiness instead of evil enchantment or death. Its inclusion of dance looks to the harmony to come and the song itself is essential to Prospero's scheme to bring Ferdinand and Miranda into love with each other. Their betrothal, which is a confirmation of love, crowns the changes that Prospero has been working for and the entertainment he conjures for them in Act IV is a demonstration of his magic art at the extreme opposite to the storm which opens the play.

Some time before this show, dancing heightens the spectacle of Act III when 'several strange Shapes' bring in a banquet, set it before the shipwrecked noblemen 'and dance about it with gentle actions of salutations; and inviting the King, &c., to eat, they depart'. All seems orderly and delightful; but when Ariel appears as a harpy and the banquet vanishes with that enigmatic 'quaint device' of the stage direction, it is because Alonso, Antonio and Sebastian are 'three men of sin'. The reappearance of the Shapes, who 'dance, with mocks and mows', and carry out the table, is a combination of dance with necessary stagecraft to make a dramatic comment: the table has to be removed, and while they are doing this, the spirits which had earlier been described by Sebastian as 'living drolleries' (i.e. puppets) now jeer at him and his fellow villains.

The spectacular confusion of this show is in contrast to the elegance and order of the betrothal entertainment, which frames the blessings of Juno and Ceres and which is also a celebration of temperance; the emphasis on chastity found in *Pericles*, *The Winter's Tale* and *Cymbeline* in *The Tempest* is both insisted upon by Prospero, and figured forth in this masque. The presenter, Iris, calls up naiads, 'cold nymphs' who wear 'chaste crowns', and 'rich Ceres', who will have nothing to do with lustful Venus and 'her blind boy's company'. These two, Iris explains, have been vanquished by the purity of the lovers; then Juno arrives and invites her 'bounteous sister' to bless the couple that they may 'prosperous be,/And honour'd in their issue' (IV. i. 104–5). Ceres, goddess of plenty, will see to this prosperity, Juno, 'highest queen of state', will ensure the honour of their family. The naiads summoned by Iris are joined by 'sun-burnt sicklemen' but their dance, the culmination of the entertainment, is surprisingly interrupted:

> Enter certain Reapers, properly habited; they join with the
> Nymphs in a graceful dance; towards the end whereof Prospero
> starts suddenly, and speaks; after which, to a strange, hollow, and
> confused noise, they heavily vanish.
>
> (IV. i. 138. 1–6)

'Gracefully' is the first descriptive word applied to dance in a
Shakespearian stage direction, and possibly indicates an insistence
that this dance should be particularly attractive and orderly so that
the interruption and departure of the performers will be the more
noticeable. The reason for this interruption – and the breaking off of
the dance and the change in the music can make a strong visual and
aural impression – is Prospero's recollection of the 'foul conspiracy/
Of the beast Caliban and his confederates' against his life. The
pleasure of courtly entertainment and the harmony of the dance
cannot continue when the wickedness of a murder plot and the
anger it arouses intrude. This unexpected ending of the dance in its
progress intensifies the meaning of a dramatic point in a way similar
to Rosaline's refusal to dance in *Love's Labour's Lost* (V. ii. 212, and
see Chapter 3) and the disappearance of the banquet earlier in *The
Tempest*. At the same time, the intrusion of evil is emphasised by the
'strange, hollow, and confused noise' which accompanies the action
and which is strictly comparable with the 'kind of hollow and
infernall musique' called for when the witches emerge from hell in
the antimasque to Jonson's *Masque of Queens* (l. 30).

Except for the descent of Juno, probably in a car drawn by
peacocks, this show presented for Miranda and Ferdinand is simple,
old-fashioned and unsophisticated when compared with the de-
veloping Jonsonian masque. In its characters and its structure it has
more affinity with the two court masques of Samuel Daniel. Iris,
Juno and Ceres all appear in Daniel's *Vision of the Twelve Goddesses*,
the Queen's masque given at Hampton Court on 8 January 1604,
and naiads dance in *Tethys' Festival*, which formed a gorgeous and
hugely expensive part of the celebrations for Prince Henry's
installation as Prince of Wales on 4 June 1610. Daniel's conception
of shows and spectacles as 'usually registred among the memorable
acts of the time, being Complements of State, both to show
magnificence and to celebrate the feasts of our greatest respects',[6] is
also apt for what Prospero calls this 'vanity of mine art'. The

appearance of the goddesses and their messenger is exactly in the tradition explained by Daniel in his letter to the Countess of Bedford which prefaces *The Vision of the Twelve Goddesses*, in which he says that the Olympian ladies have been chosen 'to serue as Hierogliphicqs for our present intention, according to some one propertie that fitted our occasion.'[7] Juno, in 'skie-colour mantle imbrodered with gold, and figured with Peacocks feathers, wearing a Crowne of gold on her head', and carrying a sceptre, 'presented the Hieroglephick of Empire and Dominion'; Ceres, 'in Strawe colour and Siluer imbrodery, with eares of Corne, and a dressing of the same', carried a sickle and represented plenty; Iris, the messenger of the goddesses, was, of course, 'dect like the Rainebow'.

Daniel's masque begins with Night awaking her son Sleep, who holds 'a blacke Wand in the left hand, to effect either confused or significant dreames', and a white in the other, which he uses 'to infuse significant visions to entertaine the Spectators'. It is very likely that Prospero also uses a staff to conjure up his show of goddesses, since he has one (v. i. 54), and he does 'infuse significant Visions to entertaine the Spectators'. The thought in the following passage from the prefatory letter to *The Vision of Twelve Goddesses* is also close to the ideas Shakespeare gives to Prospero:

> in such matters of Shewes, these like Characters (in what forme soeuer they be drawne) serue vs but to read the intention of what we would represent; as in this proiect of ours, Night & Sleepe were to produce a Vision, – an effect proper to their power, and fit to shadow our purpose, for that these apparitions & shewes are but as imaginations, and dreames that portend our affections; and dreames are neuer in all points agreeing right with waking actions.

The breaking off of the dance of nymphs and reapers in Prospero's masque is the clearest indication that his 'most majestic vision, and/ Harmonious charmingly', as Ferdinand describes it (iv. i. 118–19), is but a dream which is not 'in all points agreeing with waking actions'. The revels are ended, as he says in the play's most famous lines, and they are ended before their time. The real world does not merge with the dream world of the entertainment, as it does in the social dancing of the court masque; instead the real world (of the play) violently intrudes. It is not only the evil of the conspiracy which disturbs the dance; Prospero's anger is also a destructively discordant element. An understanding of this aspect of anger may lie behind Ariel's remark that when he had been taking part in the masque he had thought of reminding Prospero of Caliban's plot, but did not 'Lest I might anger thee' (IV. i. 169). To have done so would have meant that the show would have been ended even earlier than it had been and Ariel, who has already been threatened by his master (I. ii. 294–6) and who has the promise of freedom before him, would have no wish to arouse his wrath.

Prospero's speech on the evanescence of art and life is a superb expression of some very old ideas which are also alluded to by Jonson at the end of his masque *Love Freed from Ignorance and Folly* (1610) when he writes of Time who,

> so greedie to deuoure
> His owne, and all that hee brings forth,
> Is eating euery piece of houre
> Some obiect of the rarest worth.
>
> (ll. 362–5)

But in the thought of Prospero's speech and the show which gives rise to it Shakespeare is much nearer to Samuel Daniel than he is to the greatest writer of masques, who was contemptuous of Daniel's efforts.[8]

In *The Tempest* the 'insubstantial pageant' of the masque was presented as a waking vision. When an elaborate show with dance was included in *Henry VIII* it was presented as a dream. There are two dance scenes, both in parts of the play usually given to John Fletcher by those who hold that this great ceremonial drama is a collaborative work; but in *Henry VIII*, as in *Pericles*, dance is employed in a thoroughly Shakespearian way. The play has always been noted for its ritual, which rises and falls in six spectacles of interesting variety. In *Cymbeline* each of the major characters has a particular speech, a kind of aria; Imogen's rhapsody on receiving Posthumus's letter in III. ii, for example, Posthumus's tirade against women at the end of Act II, Iachimo's soliloquy in Imogen's bedchamber in II. ii. *Henry VIII* contains a number of similar speeches – Wolsey's farewell in III. ii, for instance – but it is the ceremonial scenes which above all else distinguish the play, and probably always have. The first of these is Cardinal Wolsey's entertainment at York Place in I. iv, and it was very probably the discharging of the small cannon announcing the disguised King's arrival at Wolsey's palace that set the Globe on fire on 29 June 1613, burning it to the ground – the greatest and most unexpected spectacle of all.

If the players were able to follow the description of the occasion in the source, Holinshed, the entry of Henry and his fellow-masquers would have been a magnificent piece of theatre.

> On a time the king came suddenlie thither in a maske with a dozen maskers all in garments like sheepheards, made of fine cloth of gold, and crimosin sattin paned, & caps of the same, with visards of good physnomie, their haires & beards either of fine gold-wire silke, or black silke, having sixteene torch-bearers, besides their drums and other persons with visards, all clothed in sattin of the same color.[9]

The scene in the play is an accurate reflection of the historical Henry's love of masques and dressing up, and his pride in his dancing and musical ability; but it was not on this occasion that he met Anne Boleyn, as the play has it. The historical date of the party at York Place was 1527, but he may have first met his future second wife as early as 1520. In March 1522 Anne was among a group of maidens 'imprisoned' in a pageant castle who were rescued by Henry in the person of 'Ardent Desire', and this was at an entertainment by Wolsey. By the time of the York Place party, the affair was well established.[10] The dramatist may be conflating the two occasions, though the first is not in Holinshed. (In any case, the scene is set dramatically in 1521, after the fall of Buckingham but before his execution.) Like similar occasions in earlier plays, this meeting of Henry and Anne in the play is emphasised by its surroundings of music and dance. In *The Tempest* Ferdinand and Miranda meet for the first time in an ambience of music, and Ariel's song may be an invitation for them to dance together. More interesting for their resemblance of thought are Romeo's words on first seeing Juliet and Henry's as he takes Anne's hand. Romeo says he will wait for Juliet to finish the measure,

> And, touching hers, make blessed my rude hand.
> Did my heart love till now? Forswear it, sight;
> For I ne'er saw true beauty till this night.
>                     (*Romeo and Juliet* I. v. 49–51)

As Henry chooses Anne as his dancing partner he says,

> The fairest hand I ever touch'd! O beauty,
> Till now I never knew thee!
>
> (I. iv. 75–6)

Unlike Romeo, Henry takes his lady into the dance and makes it an excuse to kiss her. (That she has already been kissed by Lord Sandys earlier in the scene, before the king's entrance, is an indication of her attractiveness rather than her promiscuity.)

The dance of masquers and their ladies is a vital, colourful background for the meeting and Wolsey's remark that Henry is 'with dancing a little heated', while it hints at the King's ardour, indicates that the dance has been energetic – a coranto, volta or galliard.[11] This bright, perhaps golden, scene, vigorous with life and the promise of love, is exactly balanced in the play's second half by another and very different scene with dancing, the vision of Queen Katherine. (In the Folio text, Anne is kissed by Henry at line 800; Katherine's vision appears 800 lines before the end of the play.) Other visions before death in Shakespeare are of premonitory ghosts – Richard III's on Bosworth eve, for example, or Brutus's before Philippi – but the formality of movement and symbolism of Katherine's vision are as unique as the detail of the stage direction.[12] Broken by the trial, ill and preparing to die, the Queen says to her servant,

> Good Griffith,
> Cause the musicians play me that sad note
> I nam'd my knell, whilst I sit meditating
> On that celestial harmony I go to.
>
> [*Sad and solemn music.*]

Katherine falls asleep and there appears

### The Vision

Enter, solemnly tripping one after another, six Personages clad in white robes, wearing on their heads garlands of bays, and golden vizards on their faces; branches of bays or palm in their hands. They first congee unto her, then dance; and, at certain changes, the first two hold a spare garland over her head, at which the

other four make reverent curtsies. Then the two that held the
garland deliver the same to the other next two, who observe the
same order in their changes, and holding the garland over her
head; which done, they deliver the same garland to the last two,
who likewise observe the same order; at which, as it were by
inspiration, she makes in her sleep signs of rejoicing, and holdeth
up her hands to heaven. And so in their dancing vanish, carrying
the garland with them. The music continues.

(IV. ii. 82. 1–20)

The solemnity of the dance demands a pavan-like measure and the
ritualistic action of holding the garland above Katherine's head
emphasises the symbolism so clearly expressed in the stage direction.
The word 'personages' indicates indeterminate sex, or sexlessness,
and white is of course for virtue and purity. The garlands of bay
leaves represent fame and immortality; gold stands for incorrupt-
ibility and is a Christian symbol for divine spirit and for faith
triumphant; the palm leaves which the dancers may carry could be
intended as emblems of victory over death in eternal happiness, as
they are in Revelation 7:9, where 'a great multitude . . . clothed
with white robes, and palms in their hands, praise God upon the
throne'. The palm was also an emblem of martyrdom.[13]

As this dance of the blessed spirits is the only spectacle in the play
for which there is no historical source it must be seen either as mere
embellishment or as a deliberate part of the play's dramatic
structure. If it were only decorative, the play would not suffer if the
vision and its surrounding dialogue were omitted. This is not the
case.[14] From the beginning of the play Katherine is presented as a
religious person of charitable nature. Her first action is to plead for
the common people against Wolsey's taxation; her second is to
defend Buckingham against the Cardinal's accusations. To Henry
she is at first 'saint-like' (II. iv. 138) (a description later given of
Anne at her coronation), and religious terms are used throughout
the play, and not only about or by Katherine herself. When visited
by Wolsey and Campeius after her trial, for instance, she cries out in
the midst of their insidious bullying, 'Ye have angels' faces, but
heaven knows your hearts' (III. i. 145). Angels are mentioned more
often in *Henry VIII* than in any other work in the canon, 'heaven'
occurs over forty times, and the apparition of divine spirits gives
visual expression to the ideas behind these and other religious words
in the play.

The vision also contributes to the theme of gold, which begins in the first scene when Norfolk is describing to Buckingham the meeting of Henry and the French King, Francis I, at the Field of the Cloth of Gold. The theme is developed by the familiar emblem of the sun as authority, particularly the sovereign, so that when Katherine sees the golden masks of the spirits as 'bright faces' which 'Cast thousand beams upon [her], like the sun' (IV. ii. 89) the simile has peculiar strength. It contains pathos in its significance as a symbol for Henry, from whose favour she has fallen, and glory in its prediction of the celestial life she is going to.

Like the vision in *Cymbeline*, the dream of Katherine gathers together some of the play's themes and images, but it presents them in a quietly spectacular way. The very quietness and gravity of the scene set it off from the ornate splendour of the procession for Anne's coronation which precedes it and the baptism of Elizabeth, which concludes the play. It is also subtly contrasted with the earlier dance scene, in which the gay vivacity of the dancing is preceded by the noise of cannon and after which Wolsey invites the King to a banquet 'in the next chamber'. As he takes Anne with him, Henry asks the other gentlemen to lead in their partners, saying,

> I have half a dozen healths
> To drink to these fair ladies, and a measure
> To lead 'em once again; and then lets dream
> Who's best in favour.
>
> (I. iv. 105–8)

In Act IV Scene ii the masquers are not lusty ladies and gentlemen, but incorporeal beings, and it is they who invite Katherine to a banquet. She tells Griffith,

> They promis'd me eternal happiness,
> And brought me garlands, Griffith, which I feel
> I am not worthy yet to wear. I shall, assuredly.

To which he replies,

> I am most joyful, madam, such good dreams
> Possess your fancy.
>
> (IV. ii. 90–94)

The Queen, now in disfavour with the King, dreams that she is 'best in favour', but with heaven, not with Henry. Another, and similarly direct, difference is that while Henry had been 'overheated', Katherine is 'of an earthy cold' (IV. ii. 98).

In this play of delicate constraints and balances, these correspondences and contrasts help to poise the two dance scenes in their opposition. Each is a spectacle in its own right, but as well the dancing in the first contributes to the development of the action, even more fully than the dance does in *Pericles*, and the second gives expression to the religious theme especially associated with Katherine and the imagery of gold, the sun and sovereignty. This vision shares emblematic force with the masque of *The Tempest* and even partakes of the rich complexity of the shearing festival of *The Winter's Tale*. Most of all it presents a moving image of 'that celestial harmony' Katherine is meditating upon, the order and beauty she believes she is going to after the terrible disruption of her life.

In all the last plays, as in *Timon of Athens*, dance is a more discrete element of structure than it is in the plays written before about 1607. It becomes a more specialised tool of expression, presented in relative isolation and making its dramatic point with particular emphasis. After *Pericles* the dance is less important as material for imagery and the dances themselves are more in the nature of set pieces. In no way, however, can they be considered (as they have been) to be merely extraneous pieces of spectacle included, like tumbling acts, to please the crowd.[15]

The symbolic function of dance as an emblem of order is intensified in these plays because Shakespeare draws on the elaborate techniques of the court masque. By this time the collaboration of Inigo Jones and Ben Jonson was burgeoning and the lines already being drawn for the thirty-year-long battle between Jonson's view that the masque was primarily important as a vehicle for philosophical ideas expressed in its poetry and Jones's belief that the wondrous spectacle of light, costume, and architectural design was the true glory of and reason for its being. Inigo Jones's view triumphed, only to perish along with the false ideas of greatness which it nurtured and gave such splendid expression to. With an irony that the poet himself would have appreciated Jonson's texts have survived, vindicating his attitude, while the 'baseless fabric . . . The cloud-capp'd towers, the gorgeous palaces' of Jones's invention have vanished, available to us only through the designs and sketches which have so fortunately remained.

Although the discernible influence of the masque in Shakespeare is considerable, he does not use such sophistications as dances which form geometrical figures like the 'motions circular, square, triangular' in Daniel's *Vision of the Twelve Goddesses* or 'the figure of a Diamant' in Jonson's *Masque of Beauty*, or which form letters, like one of the dances arranged by Thomas Giles for Jonson's *Masque of Queens*, which was 'graphically dispos'd into letters, and honoring the Name of the most sweete, and ingenious Prince, Charles, Duke of Yorke'.[16] But in the chivalric parade in *Pericles*, the vision of Jupiter in *Cymbeline*, the satyrs' dance in *The Winter's Tale*, the interrupted dance of naiads and reapers in *The Tempest* and the dance of the celestial spirits in *Henry VIII* (and without firm contrary evidence I believe it to be Shakespearian) the dramatist is drawing on elements of court entertainment not available to him before James ascended the throne.

# 8 Conclusions

> . . . dancing is coeval with the birth of the Universe,. and
> sprang forth at the same time with Love, the eldest of the
> gods . . . from that time the art hath been advancing, which is
> now arrived at perfection, and is at length the most muse-like,
> all comprehending, all harmonious, first of things.
>
> Lucian, 'On Dancing', translated by<br>Thomas Francklin (1781)

In the foregoing chapters I have suggested that dance is an
important element in Shakespeare's plays and that its significance is
due in particular to its value as a symbol of harmony. The dance is
used as part of the Shakespearian stage picture in a variety of ways
and far more often than the play within the play or the dumbshow.
These two pieces of stagecraft were included by.many contemporary dramatists in their plays but most of them employed
dance less often than Shakespeare or not at all.[1] When he finds
material for imagery in the dance it is almost always with full
recognition of its symbolic value so that it contributes to the theme
of a particular play or group of plays or to the presentation of the
character with which it is associated.

The four principal groups of plays Shakespeare wrote – histories,
comedies, tragedies and 'last plays', for want of a better term to
include *Henry VIII* – are distinguished almost as much by the way in
which dance and allusion to it are used as they are by their themes
and characters. The history plays, dealing in politics and the
disorder of war, especially civil war, bring no dancing on to the
stage but from the earliest dance is a basis for imagery. The
description of Jack Cade as a morris dancer in *2 Henry VI* perhaps
derives from Shakespeare's memories of country festivals; the idea of
the morris, the May-game and its mock king certainly stayed with
him during the writing of the histories up to *Henry V*. Dances of the
court also add to the stock of these images, most of which emphasise
effeminacy and artificiality as opposed to warlike courage and
action.

In comedy, which would seem to be the most natural place for dance, Shakespeare seems to be experimenting to discover how it can be used in drama – in relation to dialogue, as an influence on plot, as a believable outcome of the action. At one extreme is *A Midsummer Night's Dream*, with more dance than any other play in the canon. At another is *Love's Labour's Lost*, with (probably) no actual dancing but containing more talk of it than any other play. It is in one of the comedies that Shakespeare thoroughly integrates dance and dialogue and he ends three of them with dance as a joyous celebration of marital concord. More generally, allusions to dance, the idea of dancing and the dance itself essentially form part of the dramatic texture of the plays, adding to characterisation, illuminating the theme of order and contributing to the structure.

When the dance is used in tragedy its primarily affirmative qualities of regularity and control and its associations with love and cosmic harmony all work in counterpoint to the evil with which it becomes linked. The result is irony. Almost always dance occurs or is referred to in the earlier part of a tragedy before the theme of disorder has gained momentum.[2] The dancing and shows of two of the tragedies, *Macbeth* and *Timon of Athens*, indicate an influence from the court which was later to have even more consequence as a shaping force on Shakespeare's work. *Timon of Athens* has a special place in the development of Shakespeare's use of dance because the dancers in the masque in Act i Scene ii arrive, dance and then leave, having nothing further to do with the action. Previously every dance had included characters from the play of which it was part and the dancing had arisen with comparative informality from the plot.

In all five of the last plays dancing and allusions to it are thematically related to the tragic or near-tragic as well as to the joyful. One result of this is that Shakespeare achieved a remarkable richness of meaning for dance, particularly in *The Winter's Tale*. As well, the spectacle connected with the dancing in the last plays is greater than in those written earlier. Although the acquisition of the Blackfriars theatre by the King's Men may have contributed to this elaboration in staging, since both *Timon of Athens* and *Pericles* were written before the company began acting there a more direct influence may be found in court entertainments, especially the masques of Ben Jonson and Inigo Jones.

Shakespeare never wrote a court masque – perhaps he was never asked to – but his attitude seems to have been more in sympathy with the views of those who, like Bacon, saw masques as 'but toys', insubstantial things, however magnificent, than with Jonson's belief in their permanent value through their verse and philosophies. Jonson went to lengths to explain in some of his texts the esoteric significance of many aspects of his masques – the costumes, characters, movements – justifying what he presented by detailed reference, especially to classical authorities. How much of the significance was apparent to the performers and members of the audience cannot now be assessed but at least we know that meaning was available to them according to the degree to which they were knowledgeable. Specific details of some of Jonson's masques could be read in the printed texts which were given away as souvenirs of the performances.[3]

Shakespeare wrote at a level that was at once simpler and embraced a wider vision. Among his audiences, both courtly and common, the great commonplaces of Pythagorean and Platonic thought with their systems of cosmology and correspondences, their ideas of music and theory of numbers, were available to those whose minds were atuned, whose eyes were open and whose ears, like the ears of Pericles, were unstopped. He was thus able to use the dance as a visual image of harmony and order in the world, and it is a movement towards that harmony, that resolution of disorder, which is the essential basis of his plays.

# Glossary of Dance Terms

(Dates in brackets refer to the earliest use cited in *O.E.D.*)

| | |
|---|---|
| Almain (alman, almayn) | Sedate, stately dance with four beats to the bar, lightened by the introduction of small hopping steps. (1549) |
| Bergomask (bergamask) | Clownish rustic dance named after a dance from the Bergamo district in Lombardy, where the peasants were supposedly rude and clumsy. The true bergomask is a ring dance, usually rather fast and in duple time. (1590) |
| Basse dance (Fr., low dance) | A rather solemn dance usually in duple time, without any jumps. Widespread in the Middle Ages, it seems to have developed into the pavan. (Not in *O.E.D.* in this sense.) |
| Brawl (branle, bransle, braul and other forms) | (a) Step in the basse dance which appears to have been a rocking step in which the body remains on one spot but the weight is moved from one foot to the other. The precise interpretation has aroused much discussion. (1521) |
| | (b) Linked dance related to the basse dance, usually in duple time; the dancers move sideways instead of forward. Thoinot Arbeau gives directions for twenty-four different branles in *Orchesography* (1589) and there were many others. (1541) |

| | |
|---|---|
| Canary (canarie, canaries) | Sprightly, jigging dance, usually in $\frac{3}{8}$ or $\frac{6}{8}$ time, said by some to have originated in the Canary Isles and travelled to England and France through Spain. (1592) |
| Caper | (a) Frolicking leap. (1592) In the morris dance, a particularly high spring. In the galliard a high spring during which the dancer rapidly moves his feet. |
| | (b) To make such a leap. (1588) |
| Carole (carol) | (a) Ring dance to an accompaniment sung usually by the dancers themselves. (1300) |
| | (b) To perform such a dance. (1300) |
| Change | Finite passage of a dance, apparently equivalent to a strain in music in the sense of 'a musical idea or passage, more or less complete in itself'. (1588) See *O.E.D.*, Change, sb. 1. c. and strain, sb². III. 11. |
| Cinquepace | See 'galliard'. (1590) |
| Coranto | (Fr., courante, running dance). A light, quick dance usually in triple time, and characterised by little hops or springs, resulting in a skipping step. (1564) |
| Double | Basic dance movement in which one foot advances, is joined by the other which then pauses while the first moves forward again, to be once more joined by the second, with the heels together. (1531) |
| Fleuret | Galliard movement combining three small steps without a high leap: a flourish. (1677) |
| Galliard | A lively dance in triple time with leaping steps and intricate variations; often danced after a pavan. Also called the cinquepace or sinkapace from the French cinq pas (five steps), referring |

to the five steps which are danced to six beats, the fifth being without a step. The most popular quick court dance for couples in the sixteenth century, it also gave special opportunity for virtuoso solo displays by men dancers. (1530)

**Hay**

(a) Dance figure in which the performer moves in and out between other dancers in sequence. The term may derive from French *haye*, the name for an artificial hedge made of upright stakes interlaced transversely with thin strips or stems. (Not in *O.E.D.* in this sense.)

(b) Winding dance characterised by this figure. (1529)

**Honour**

Bow (man) or curtsy (woman) usually made at the beginning and end of a dance but sometimes as part of a figure within the dance itself. (1531). 'Reverence' (1393) was also used and 'congee', which originally referred to leave-taking at the end. (1586)

**Hornpipe**

Vigorous country dance accompanied by a wind instrument; since the nineteenth century associated especially with sailors. (1485)

**Jig (ieig, iyg, iigge and other forms)**

(a) Any lively, springy kind of dance. (1560)

(b) Dance and song of a bright and apparently bawdy nature at the end of a play. (1592)

**Lavolta (lavolto, volt, volta)**

Fast and energetic dance in triple time, in which the men lift their partners in the air as they turn. It is related to the galliard and was a favourite of Queen Elizabeth I. (1584)

**Longways**

Formation of dancers in two files, partners usually facing each other; a country dance term. (1588, though not related to dancing specifically.)

Matachins
    (a) Dance representing a mock battle with the 'combatants' wearing armour and wielding swords. (1586)
    (b) Sword dance related to the morris. (Not in *O.E.D.* strictly in this sense.)

Measure
    (a) Stately, grave dance; the word seems also to have come to be synonymous with pavan, especially when used in the plural. (1584, but perhaps also 1509.) 'The measures' were a regular part of the revels after a masque and were danced on festive days at the Inns of Court. The word has given rise to much discussion.
    (b) Section of a dance. [Not in *O.E.D.* in this sense, but perhaps related to Measure, sb. 18 b. Each portion of a musical composition comprising a group of notes beginning with a main accent and commonly included between two vertical lines or bars; a 'bar'. (1667)]

Morisco
    (a) Morris dance. (1561)
    (b) Morris dancer. (1593)

Morris (moreys, morrice and many other forms)
    (a) Grotesque dance in which the performers wear fancy costumes. (1458) Specifically an English folk dance in which the performers wear bells on their legs and the dance sometimes includes such extra characters as Maid Marian, a fool and a hobby-horse. Sometimes one dancer has a blackened face.
    (b) Group of grotesque dancers, or morris dancers. (1500–20) (The

origin and early meaning of the word are obscure.)

| | |
|---|---|
| Passing measure pavan | Type of pavan for which the music was a melody played over one of two sixteen-measure bass lines; *passamezzo antico* was in the minor mode and *passamezzo moderno* in the major. (The term has occasioned much discussion.) |
| Pavan (pavane, pavin, pavyon and other forms) | Usually a grave, stately dance in duple time; danced as a processional opening to balls and on other solemn occasions. It appears to have developed from the basse dance and many variations were current, some of them relatively quick. (1530). |
| Round | (a) Formation of dancers in a circle, hands linked or unlinked. (1590) <br> (b) Dance in such a formation. (1513) |
| Ruade | Movement in the galliard in which the dancer kicks one leg behind, bending it at the knee. (Not in *O.E.D.*) |
| Sinkapace | See 'galliard'. |
| Single (simple) | Basic dance movement in which one foot moves forward and the other is brought up beside it, with the heels together. (1531) |
| Trick | Variation in a galliard, perhaps of a particularly dextrous kind. (Not in *O.E.D.* in this sense, but probably related to Trick, sb. 5. A feat of dexterity or skill, intended to surprise or amuse; a piece of jugglery or leger-demain. (1606)) |

# Notes

1. John Nichols, *The Progresses . . . of Queen Elizabeth* (London, 1788), ii, 'Queen Elizabeth's Plate and Jewels', p. 41.
2. J. R. Tanner, *Constitutional Documents of the Reign of James I* (Cambridge, 1961), p. 15.
3. See Roy Strong, *Splendour at Court* (London, 1973) and Roy Strong and Stephen Orgel, *Inigo Jones* (London, 1973).
4. The subject is treated exhaustively in S. K. Heninger Jr, *Touches of Sweet Harmony* (San Marino, 1974), which contains an extensive bibliography.
5. John Dee, Preface to Henry Billingsley's *Elements of Geometrie* (1570), p. 2.
6. Robert Burton, *The Anatomy of Melancholy*, ed. F. Dell and P. Jordan-Smith (New York, 1938), p. 710.
7. Thoinot Arbeau, *Orchesography*, trans. C. W. Beaumont (London, 1925), pp. 162–3.
8. Edmund Lodge, *Illustrations of British History . . .* (London, 1838) (repr. 1969), ii, 386.
9. A. H. de Maisse, *Journal*, trans. G. B. Harrison and R. A. Jones (London, 1931), p. 95.
10. The names of dances and dance terms are explained in the Glossary of Dance Terms at the end of the book.
11. See Paul Reyher, *Les Masques Anglais* (Paris, 1909) (repr. 1964), p. 439, and *C. S. P. Dom., Eliz. 1601–03* (London, 1870) (repr. 1967), p. 179.
12. Arbeau, *Orchesography*, trans. Mary Stewart Evans (New York, 1967), p. 59. Mrs C. H. Bright has drawn my attention to what appears to be a survival of this practice in the Philippines, where at important balls the general dancing does not begin until the highest officials and their guests have circled the floor in a rigadoon.
13. See Eric St John Brooks, *Sir Christopher Hatton* (London, 1947), p. 31.
14. See Gerard Legh, *Accedens of Armory* (1562), ff. 204–13, and Marie Axton, 'Robert Dudley and the Inner Temple Revels', *Hist. Jnl*, 13 (1970), 365–70, in which it is suggested that these revels were intended to further Dudley's matrimonial intentions with the Queen.
15. See J. P. Cunningham, *Dancing in the Inns of Court* (London, 1965).
16. Bodl. MS Douce 208, fo. 195$^v$.
17. Quoted by Cunningham, op. cit., p. 9.
18. See Richard Mulcaster, *Positions*, ed. R. H. Quick (London, 1888), p. 75; Roger Ascham, *The Schoolmaster* (1573), p. 19; Baldassare Castiglione, *The Book of the Courtier*, trans. Sir Thomas Hoby, ed. W. E. Henley (London, 1900), pp. 370, 116.

19. Sir Thomas Elyot, *The Book named the Governor*, ed. S. E. Lehmberg (London, 1962), p. 62. His discussion of the dance is on pp. 62–85 of this edition. See also John M. Major, 'The Moralization of the Dance in Elyot's *Governor*', *Studies in the Renaissance*, v (1958), 27–36.

20. Coplande's instructions exist in a unique copy in the Bodleian Library. They have been reprinted several times, and a good summary of discussion about them is found in John M. Ward, 'The maner of dauncyng', *Early Music*, 4 (1976), 127–42.

21. *Rich's Farewell to Military Profession*, ed. Thomas M. Cranfell (Austin, 1959), pp. 4–5.

22. *Cal. of Patent Rolls, Eliz. 1* (26 Feb 1574) (London, 1973), vi, § 1381.

23. Leslie Hotson, *The First Night of Twelfth Night* (London, 1961), p. 171.

24. Desiderius Erasmus, *The Education of a Christian Prince*, trans. Lester K. Born (New York, 1965), p. 246.

25. Juan Luis Vives, *Linguae Latinae Exercitatio*, trans. Forster Watson (London, 1970), pp. 172–3.

26. Ibid., p. 184.

27. Quoted by Sir E. Brydges and J. Haslewood, *The British Bibliographer*, IV (1813), 225.

28. Christopher Fetherston, *A Dialogue agaynst . . . dauncing* (1582), sig. B.

29. See John Northbrooke, *A Treatise wherein Dicing, Dauncing, Vaine playes or Enterluds . . . are reproued*, [1577?], ed. J. P. Collier (London, 1843), pp. 170–7; Stephen Gosson, *The School of Abuse* (1579), ed. J. P. Collier (London, 1841; Shakes. Soc.), pp. 24–5, 35; Philip Stubbes, *The Anatomy of Abuses* (1583), ed. F. S. Furnivall (London, 1877–82; New Shakes. Soc.), esp. pp. 154–6. A late flowering of such ranting can be found in William Prynne's *Histriomastix* (1633), esp. pp. 220–53.

30. John Case, *The Praise of Musicke* (1586), p. 79.

31. D. [sic] Rainoldes, *Ouerthrow of Stage-Plays* (1629), p. 17.

32. John Field, *A Godly Exhortation, by occasion of the late iudgement of God, showed at Paris Garden* (1583).

33. The source for quotations from Shakespeare's plays is *The Complete Works*, ed. Peter Alexander (London, 1951), in which the lines are numbered as in the Cambridge edition of Clark and Wright.

34. See E. K. Chambers, *The Elizabethan Stage* (Oxford, 1928), ii, 564. Platter later uses the cognate, 'zierlichsten', to describe the actors' expensive clothes which have been bequeathed to them by noblemen; Chambers has several references to jigs at ii, 551. The standard reference is Charles Baskervill, *The Elizabethan Jig* (Chicago, 1929).

35. In the Preface to his *View of France* (1598), quoted in W. B. Rye, *England as Seen by Foreigners* (London, 1865), p. xxiii.

36. On masques in plays see Inga-Stina Ewbank, 'These Pretty Devices', in *A Book of Masques*, gen. ed. T. J. B. Spencer (Cambridge, 1966), pp. 407–49.

37. For teaching the dances in *Love Freed from Ignorance and Folly*, given at court on 3 February 1611, Jonson and Jones were each paid £40; the dancing masters Bochan and Confess were paid, respectively, £20 and £50. See E. K. Chambers, ibid., iii, 387.

38. Royal interest went further than merely watching. King James owned copies of the two principal Italian dance treatises, Fabritio Caroso's *Della Nobiltà di*

*Dame* (Venice, 1600) and Cesare Negri's *Nuove Inventione di Balli* (Milan, 1604), both now in the British Library. Prince Henry also owned a copy of Caroso, and he and Prince Charles were applauded for their dancing skill.

## CHAPTER 2

1. J. Payne Collier, *Annals of the Stage* (London, 1831), additional notes, p. xviii, cited by Barbara Lowe, 'Early Records of the Morris in England', *Journal of the English Folk Dance and Song Society*, viii, 2 (1957), 62. The earliest reference to a morris dance found by Lowe is in 1458.
2. See *Shakespeare, Plays and Poems*, ed. James Boswell (London, 1821), xviii, 250–1; *2 Henry VI*, ed. Andrew S. Cairncross (London, 1962), p. 78. On the morris dance and the derivation of the word 'morris' see Cecil J. Sharp and Herbert C. MacIlwaine, *The Morris Book*, 2nd edn. (London, 1912–19), i, 7–75; E. K. Chambers, *The Medieval Stage* (Oxford, 1925), i, 195–204.
3. *Old Meg of Hereford-shire for a Mayd Marian: And Hereford Towne for a Morris-daunce* (1609), sig. B4.
4. See Lowe, op. cit., p. 64.
5. See Sharp, op. cit., p. 31.
6. Ibid., p. 54.
7. Ibid., p. 12 and Chambers, op. cit., i, 132–3.
8. Froissart, *The Chronicle of Froissart*, trans. Lord Berners (London, 1903), vi, 374, describes the fate of the four alleged murderers of Thomas of Woodstock in 1397.
9. See W. B. Rye, *England as Seen by Foreigners* (London, 1865), p. 9.
10. In his note to lines 12–13 in the Cambridge edition (1968), John Dover Wilson suggests 'i.e. he (the warrior) dances to the accompaniment of the pleasantly lascivious lute. Prob. alluding to the amorous Ed. IV'; Wolfgang Clemen agrees that the *he* refers to a 'hypothetical soldier, with a possible hint at Edward IV' (*A Commentary on Shakespeare's 'Richard III'* (London, 1968), pp. 2–3). The text clearly has 'Grim-visag'd war' as the noun for which 'he' is the pronoun; there is no need to postulate a hypothetical warrior.
11. For a discussion of the garden scene and further references see Peter Ure's introduction to the New Arden edition of the play (London, 1961), pp. li–lvii. On the play's imagery generally, see especially. Wolfgang Clemen, *The Development of Shakespeare's Imagery* (London, 1951), and Richard Altick, 'Symphonic Imagery in *Richard II*', *PMLA*, lxii (1947), 339–65.
12. See M. P. Tilley, *A Dictionary of the Proverbs in England . . .* (Ann Arbor, 1950), p. 69, B695, and notes by Matthew Black in the New Variorum edition (Philadelphia, 1955), p. 266 and Peter Ure in the New Arden edition (London, 1961), p. 136.
13. *PMLA*, lxii (1947), 339–65.
14. The relationship between Shakespeare's presentation of Henry as a Christian prince and the ideas of Erasmus (not including dancing) are discussed by J. H. Walter in his Introduction to the New Arden edition of the play (London, 1954), pp. xvii–xviii.
15. Sharp, op. cit., p. 28. See also p. 21 and, on May-games, Chambers, op. cit., ch. viii.

CHAPTER 3

1. Helen Gardner, *More Talking About Shakespeare*, ed. John Garrett (London, 1959), p. 23; Enid Welsford, *The Court Masque* (Cambridge, 1927), p. 334; A. P. Rossiter, *Angel with Horns* (London, 1961), pp. 68, 76; John Russell Brown, *Shakespeare and His Comedies* (London, 1957), p. 139.

2. H. Granville-Barker, *Prefaces to Shakespeare* (London, 1958), ii, 426, 448.

3. Cited in *Love's Labour's Lost*, ed. R. David (London, 1951), p. 21.

4. As C. L. Barber does in *Shakespeare's Festive Comedy* (Princeton, N.J., 1959), pp. 119–62.

5. Robert Kirk, *Secret Commonwealth* (Edinburgh, 1815), p. 8.

6. Ibid., p. 4.

7. See e.g. J. D. Wilson, *Shakespeare's Happy Comedies* (London, 1962), pp. 191–207, and, for a more circumspect view, Stanley Wells' introduction to the Penguin edition of the play (Harmondsworth, 1968).

8. Elyot, *The Book named the Governor*, ed. S. E. Lehmberg (London, 1962), p.77.

9. See Melusine Wood, *Some Historical Dances* (London, 1952), pp. 11ff.

10. See Agnes de Mille, *The Book of the Dance* (London, 1963), p. 44.

11. Thomas Nashe, *The Terrors of the Night* (1594), sig. B2v.

12. See e.g. *The Merry Wives of Windsor*, ed. H. C. Hart (London, 1904), p. 211; Robert Burton, *The Anatomy of Melancholy* (New York, 1938), p. 168.

13. The Royal Shakespeare Company's 1968 production added to the pagan atmosphere by dressing Falstaff in a furry coat so that he resembled an animal even more closely; presumably to escape the fairies he climbed into the oak tree, but this made him in effect the high priest of the revels, both celebrant and victim.

14. John Dennis, *The Comical Gallant* (London, 1702), sig. A2. Cited in *The Merry Wives of Windsor*, ed. H. J. Oliver (London, 1971), p. xiv.

15. See Leslie Hotson, *Shakespeare versus Shallow* (London, 1931), pp. 111–22; William Green, *Shakespeare's 'Merry Wives of Windsor'* (Princeton, N.J., 1962), pp. 21–50; and G. R. Hibbard (ed.), *The Merry Wives of Windsor* (Harmondsworth, 1973), pp. 46–53. See also John M. Steadman, 'Falstaff as Actaeon: A Dramatic Emblem', *Shakespeare Quarterly*, 14 (1963) 231–44, where it is suggested that Falstaff's amorous misadventures are dramatic *exempla* of the Garter motto.


CHAPTER 4

1. In the first Quarto of *Much Ado About Nothing*, three speeches are given to Bene[dick] and two to Balth[asar] in the conversation between Margaret and the gentleman (II. i. 86–96). If it were Benedick who began dancing with Margaret, he would have to leave her halfway through the figure, about l. 92, in order to get to Beatrice; this seems improbable as no other exchanges of partners are made. Although Dover Wilson and C. J. Sisson agree that Borachio is the most likely partner for Margaret (see Sisson's *New Readings in Shakespeare*, 2 vols, Cambridge, 1956, i, 100), Borachio, 'a lewd fellow' (v. i. 136), a drunkard (III. iii. 98) and a perfumer of rooms (I. iii. 51) who is a companion of the melancholy Don John, is far less likely to take part in

dancing than Balthasar, who is musical, and a personal attendant on Don Pedro, Prince of Arragon, just as Margaret is an attendant on Hero, the daughter of Messina's Governor. See Alan Brissenden, ' "Much Ado About Nothing", 1. ii. 86–96: The Case for Balthasar', *Notes and Queries*, n.s. 26, 2 (1979), 116–17.

2. Bodl. MS Rawl., d. 864 fo. 199.
3. In Tyrone Guthrie's production of *All's Well That Ends Well*, which was in the opening season of the Shakespeare Festival in Stratford, Ontario in 1953, Helena and the King made a dancing entrance, and Helena later danced with the lords when the King asked her to make her choice among them. In Guthrie's production for the Melbourne Theatre Company in 1969, there was no dancing entrance, but each of the lords had a short dance as Helena came to them, and she finished by waltzing a few steps with Bertram. John Barton's Royal Shakespeare Company production of 1968 brought Helena and the King dancing on to the stage, but extended the visual image no further.
4. Thomas Morley, *A Plaine and Easie Introduction to Practicall Musicke* (1597), p. 181; Arbeau, op. cit., p. 123.
5. Arbeau, op. cit., p. 180. See also p. 39 above.
6. A hay is suggested by John H. Long in his *Shakespeare's Use of Music* (Gainesville, 1955), p. 160.
7. Anne Barton, ' "As You Like It" and "Twelfth Night": Shakespeare's Sense of an Ending', *Shakespearian Comedy*, ed. Malcolm Bradbury and David Palmer (London, 1972), p. 167.
8. Ibid., p. 166.
9. See Leslie Hotson, *The First Night of Twelfth Night* (London, 1961), pp. 167–72, and T. W. Craik's notes in the New Arden edition of *Twelfth Night* (London, 1975), pp. 153–6.
10. R. A. Foakes, 'Voices of Maturity in Shakespeare's Comedies', in *Shakespearian Comedy*, ed. Malcolm Bradbury and David Palmer (London, 1972), p. 136.
11. W. R. Prest, *The Inns of Court* (London, 1972), p. 154.
12. See Arbeau, op. cit., pp. 78–9.
13. See Otto Gombosi, 'Some Musical Aspects of the English Court Masque', *Jnl of Am. Musicol. Soc.*, i, 3 (1948), 14, and F.W. Sternfeld, *Music in Shakespearian Tragedy* (Oxford, 1962), pp. 250–2.
14. See H. H. Furness (ed.), *Twelfth Night or, What You Will* (New York, 1964 (repr. edn. of 1901)), pp. 297–8. See also the notes to the New Arden edition, ed. J. M. Lothian and T. W. Craik (London, 1975), pp. 141–2.
15. See Hotson, op. cit., Ch. v.
16. Philip Stubbes, *The Anatomie of Abuses* (1583), ed. F. S. Furnivall (London, 1877–82; New Shakes. Soc.), pp. 154, 155, 156.
17. See also Ian Donaldson, '*All's Well That Ends Well*: Shakespeare's Play of Endings', *Essays in Criticism*, xxvii, 1 (1977), 34–55.

CHAPTER 5

1. Luigi da Porto, *Hystoria Nouellamente* . . . (Venice, n.d.), sig. Avi. See also O. H. Moore, *The Legend of Romeo and Juliet* (Columbus, 1950), pp. 131, 138.
2. Ficino, *Sopra l' Amore o Vero Convito di Platone* (Florence, 1594), p. 23. (Translated from J. Vyvyan, *Shakespeare and Platonic Beauty* (London, 1961), p. 39.)

3. Castiglione, *The Book of the Courtier*, trans. Sir Thomas Hoby (London, 1900), p. 356.
4. See e.g. C. F. E. Spurgeon, *Shakespeare's Imagery* (Cambridge, 1935), pp. 310–16, and M. Mahood, *Shakespeare's Wordplay* (London, 1957), pp. 66–8.
5. Lucian, *The Dance*, trans. A. M. Harmon (London, 1934) (Loeb Classical Library, *Lucian*, v) p. 221. Doubt has been cast on Lucian's authorship of this dialogue. See Margaret McGowan, *L'Art du ballet de cour* . . . (Paris, 1963), p. 14 n. 19, cited by Julia Sutton, Arbeau, op. cit., p. 209.
6. Arthur Brooke, *The Tragicall History of Romeus and Juliet*, ed. P. A. Daniel (London, 1875), l. 246.
7. See Alan Brissenden, 'Shakespeare and the Morris', *Review of English Studies*, n.s., xxx, 117 (1979), 1–11.
8. For examples of diverse views, see W. C. Curry, Shakespeare's *Philosophical Patterns* (Baton Rouge, 1937); H. N. Paul, *The Royal Play of Macbeth* (New York, 1950); M. C. Bradbrook, 'The Sources of *Macbeth*', *Shakespeare Survey*, 4 (1951), 35–48; and M. D. W. Jeffreys, 'The Weird Sisters in *Macbeth*', *English Studies in Africa*, i (1958), 43–54, 229–35.
9. Sir John Davies, *Poems*, ed. Robert Krueger (Oxford, 1975), p. 110.
10. See Edgar Wind, *Pagan Mysteries in the Renaissance* (London, 1958), pp. 31–56.
11. Seneca, *De Beneficiis*, trans. Arthur Golding (London, 1578), fo. 3ᵛ.
12. Servius, *In Vergilii Aeneidem*, i, 720, quoted by Wind, *Pagan Mysteries in the Renaissance*, p. 33. For a dissident view see N. Comes, *Mythologie*, trans. I. de Montlyard (Lyon, 1607), p. 384.
13. See Wind, *Pagan Mysteries in the Renaissance*, p. 34.
14. Seneca, *De Beneficiis*, op. cit.
15. As in e.g. 'They danced along the Kirk-yeard . . . and John Fein mussiled [i.e. masked] led the ring . . . The men turned nine times Widder-shines about, and the Women six times'. George Sinclair, *Satan's Invisible World Discovered* (Edinburgh, 1685), p. 25. The numbers are multiples of three.
16. 'At wch, wth a strange and sodayne Musique, they fell into a *magicall Daunce*, full of praeposterous change, and gesticulation, but most applying to theyr property: who, at theyr meetings, do all thinges contrary to the custome of Men, dauncing, back to back, hip to hip, theyr handes joyn'd, and making theyr *circles* backward to the left hand, wth strange phantastique motions of theyr heads, and bodyes. All wch were excellently imitated by the Maker of the Daunce, Mr. Hierome Herne, whose right it is, here to be name'd.' Ben Jonson, *The Masque of Queens*, ll. 344–53. (*Ben Jonson*, eds. C. H. Herford and P. and E. Simpson (Oxford, 1947), vii, 301.
17. See *Macbeth*, ed. Kenneth Muir (London, 1962), p. 111.
18. See *Shakespeare's Plutarch*, ed. T. J. B. Spencer (Harmondsworth, 1964), p. 214.
19. See M. R. Ridley's note to this passage in the New Arden edition of the play (London, 1967).
20. John Chamberlain, *Letters*, ed. Norman E. McClure (Philadelphia, 1939), ii, 41.
21. See the account in G. B. Harrison, *A Jacobean Journal* (London, 1946), p. 325.
22. The best summary of discussion on the date of composition is in J. C. Maxwell's introduction to his edition of the play (Cambridge, 1957), pp. xi–xiv.
23. See Frances A. Yates, *The Valois Tapestries* (London, 1975), pp. 45, 62.
24. *Ben Jonson*, op. cit., p. 306.

25. Philip Sidney, *The Countesse of Pembrokes Arcadia* (1590), ff. 63, 63ᵛ.
26. Rabelais, *The Heroic Deeds of Gargantua and Pantagruel*, II, xxvi (London, 1951), p. 232.
27. A direction not noticed by Walter Sorell, who suggests that they may have performed a sword dance. See 'Shakespeare and the Dance', *Shakespeare Quarterly*, viii (1957), 373.
28. Stephen Orgel and Roy Strong, op. cit., i. 46.
29. David Cook, '*Timon of Athens*', *Shakespeare Survey*, 16 (1963), 85.
30. A. S. Collins, '*Timon of Athens: A Reconsideration*', *Review of English Studies*, xxii (1946), 97. Inga-Stina Ewbank suggests that the masque in *Timon of Athens* represents perhaps 'the most far-reaching use of the masque as social symbol' ('These Pretty Devices', *A Book of Masques*, gen. ed. T. J. B. Spencer, (Cambridge, 1966), p. 418.)

## CHAPTER 6

1. See the surveys of criticism of the last plays by Philip Edwards in *Shakespeare Survey*, 11 (1958), and *Shakespeare*, ed. Stanley Wells (Oxford, 1973). More recent criticism which is relevant includes Howard Felperin, *Shakespearean Romance* (Princeton, N.J., 1972), Hallett Smith, *Shakespeare's Romances* (San Marino, 1972), and Frances Yates, *Shakespeare's Last Plays* (London, 1975). On *Macbeth* and King James see the work of H. N. Paul and M. C. Bradbrook referred to in note 8 to Chapter 5.
2. An event which some scholars see as decisive for the form and content of the last plays. The theory is somewhat weakened by *Pericles* having been performed before the King's Men began acting in the Blackfriars. See G. E. Bentley, 'Shakespeare and the Blackfriars Theatre', *Shakespeare Survey*, 1 (1948), 38–50, and Allardyce Nicoll's *caveat*, 'Shakespeare and the Court Masque', *Shakespeare Jahrbuch*, xciv (1958), 51–62. On the authorship and date of *Pericles* see particularly F. D. Hoeniger's introduction to the New Arden edition (London, 1963) and Philip Edwards's to the Penguin edition (Harmondsworth, 1973).
3. The picture is reproduced and excellently described in S. K. Heninger, Jr, op. cit., pp. 184–5.
4. Hoeniger notes that 'similar scenes are not uncommon in Elizabethan drama' (New Arden edition, p. 52), and includes *Troilus and Cressida* in the list. Five plays in twenty-five years is hardly common, however, and in *Troilus and Cressida* i. ii there is merely a parade of knights, with no ceremonial concerning shields. Marston introduces a masque, with impresas, in *The Insatiate Countess* (c. 1610).
5. See Frances Yates, 'Elizabethan Chivalry: The Romance of the Accession Day Tilts', *Journal of the Warburg and Courtauld Institutes*, xx, 1 (1957), 4–25. Roy Strong, 'Inigo Jones and the Revival of Chivalry', *Apollo*, lxxxvi (1967), 102–7, and Stephen Orgel and Roy Strong, *Inigo Jones* (London, 1973), i, 179–89.
6. See *O.E.D.* Matachin, 2. a., E. K. Chambers, *Elizabethan Stage*, iii, 280, and Arbeau, op. cit., pp. 183, 210, 213.
7. Geoffrey Bullough, *Narrative and Dramatic Sources of Shakespeare*, vi (London, 1966), 389.
8. Ibid., p. 438. Bullough notes that II. v. 25–8 suggests that Pericles also played an instrument.

9. George Wilkins, *The Painfull Aduentures of Pericles Prince of Tyre*, ed. Kenneth Muir (Liverpool, 1967), p. 40.

10. G. Wilson Knight musters a great many relationships with other plays to bolster his defence of Shakespeare's authorship of the vision scene. See *The Crown of Life* (London, 1961), pp. 168–202.

11. Granville-Barker thinks that the apparitions stand around Posthumus and that the music is played offstage, as the direction 'cannot imply attendant apparitions performing upon recorders'. To 'circle round' strongly implies movement (*O.E.D.*, Circle, *v.* 4., considers 'To form a circle; to stand or extend in a circle' rare and cites 1613–16 as its earliest use); there is no reason that the music could not have been played on stage and instruments other than recorders used – the ladies in Timon's masque play lutes, though admittedly wind instruments often accompany supernatural appearances on the contemporary stage. (See Harley Granville-Barker, *Prefaces to Shakespeare*, Second Series (London, 1947), p. 254.) Arbeau says, 'Pavans are also used in masquerades to herald the entrance of the gods and goddesses in their triumphal chariots or emperors and kings in full majesty.' (Op. cit., p. 59.)

12. See G. E. Bentley, *The Jacobean and Caroline Stage* (Oxford, 1956), iv, 1231 and E. K. Chambers, *William Shakespeare* (Oxford, 1963), ii, 352.

13. The two pictures are reproduced in Stephen Orgel and Roy Strong, op. cit., ii, 478, 483.

14. According to some sources Harmonia, or Harmony, was born of the union of Ares, god of war, and Aphrodite, goddess of love. Others say she was the daughter of Zeus and Electra, the daughter of Atlas. (See *Larousse Encyclopedia of Mythology* (London, 1960), pp. 107, 138, and Alastair Fowler, 'Leontes' Contrition and the Repair of Nature', *Essays and Studies*, n. s. 31 (London, 1978), p. 38.)

15. See above, Chapter 2.

16. Walter Sorell notes that in the *Arcadia* Sidney mentions a dance by two groups of shepherds 'as it were in a brawle' (*Shakespeare Quarterly*, viii (1957), 380). See note 23.

17. See Chapter 3 above, pp. 39 and Arbeau, op. cit., 128–72.

18. *The Winter's Tale*, ed. J. H. P. Pafford (London, 1967), p. 101.

19. See *The Winter's Tale*, ed. H. H. Furness (1898, repr. New York, 1964), pp. 223–4.

20. For a dissenting view, see *Cymbeline*, ed. J. C. Maxwell (Cambridge, 1960), pp. xi–xii.

21. See *Ben Jonson*, eds Herford and Simpson (Oxford, 1950), x, 519–22.

22. *Essays and Studies* (1978), p. 58.

23. See Andrew Sabol, *Songs and Dances for the Stuart Masques* (Providence, 1959), p. 169, the same author's *Four Hundred Songs and Dances from the Stuart Masque* (Providence, 1978), p. 12, and J. H. P. Pafford's note to IV. iv. 343 in the New Arden edition, suggesting that the dance in the play was probably a brawl or branle and referring to Sorell's article in *Shakespeare Quarterly*, viii (1957). It is clear from Jonson's description that the dance of satyrs in *Oberon* was grotesque, with wild leaps and outlandish gestures, very different from the orderly brawl that may have been danced by the shepherds and shepherdesses earlier in the scene. The error has probably arisen from the frequent contemporary punning on brawl = quarrel and brawl = dance, as in *Love's Labour's Lost* III. i. 8, which I think is also used by Jonson in *Oberon* itself, where

one of the satyrs says 'let vs fall/To a song, or to a brawle' (ll. 251–2); the word is being used here generically, as 'measure' often is, probably as a pun to mean 'quarrel' in opposition to 'song', and for sake of the rhyme. The context of the passage in Sidney alluded to by Sorell specifically opposes a dance by the shepherds which is wild and 'made a right picture of their chiefe god Pan, and his companions the Satyres' and a dance done hand in hand 'as it were in a braule', performed to a song about love and music, which does not 'moue kindly without loue'. (*Arcadia*, 1590, fo. 86.)

24. When St Paul the first hermit (not the apostle) who lived in the third century A. D. set off on his travels to find a man better than himself he met a centaur and then a satyr on the way; according to his biographer, St Jerome, both were the devil in disguise. See E. K. Rand, *Founders of the Middle Ages* (New York, 1957), p. 123.

25. Vincenzo Cartari, *Le Imagini de i Dei de gli Antichi* (Venice, 1571, reprinted New York, 1976), p. 140 (translation by Robin Eaden). Satyrs are also discussed in several bestiaries, including Edward Topsell's *Historie of Foure-Footed Beastes* (1607), pp. 12–15.

26. See Stephen Orgel, *The Jonsonian Masque* (Cambridge, Mass., 1965), especially pp. 72–3, 82–6, and Roy Strong, *Splendour at Court* (London, 1973), pp. 216–20. For a penetrating discussion of dance in Jonsonian masque see John C. Meagher, *Method and Meaning in Jonson's Masques* (Notre Dame, Indiana, 1966), Ch. IV.

27. This analysis had been written before I read R. A. Foakes's brief but similar interpretation in *Shakespeare: From the Dark Comedies to the Last Plays* (London, 1971), pp. 132–3. It was pleasing to find my ideas corroborated by those of Professor Foakes.

CHAPTER 7

1. The culprit seems to have been Steevens, who claimed in his note that kissing 'was anciently done at the beginning of some dances' [*The Plays of William Shakespeare* (London, 1805), i, 27]. See also notes in the New Variorum (Philadelphia, 1892, pp. 77–80), and New Arden (London, 1962, p. 34) editions.

2. See Bodl. MSS Rawl. d. 864 ff. 119$^v$ and Rawl. Poet. ff. 10$^v$–11.

3. John Playford, *The English Dancing Master* (London, 1652), p. 1. The text has been modernised. See also E. K. Chambers, *The Elizabethan Stage*, i, 198.

4. Steevens' note that 'a kiss was anciently the established fee of a lady's partner' [*The Plays of William Shakespeare* (London, 1778), vii, 215] is highly suspect as his supporting quotation is taken from a virulent anti-dance pamphlet, *A Dialogue Betweene Custom and Veritie concerning the Vse and Abuse of Dancing and Minstrelsie* (1581), and needs to be read in its context. This quotation from *Henry VIII* has been continually used since Steevens' day, and not only by Shakespearian scholars, to support the idea that kissing after, and even before, a dance was 'customary'. W. B. Rye, for example, mentions kissing as being common in social life (which it was) but then quotes these words of Shakespeare's *Henry VIII* as evidence that kissing 'appears to have been the customary fee of a lady's partner' [*England as Seen by Foreigners* (London, 1865), p. 262].

5. Penguin edition (Harmondsworth, 1968), p. 149.
6. Samuel Daniel, *Complete Works*, ed. A. B. Grosart (Blackburn, 1885), iii, 305.
7. Ibid., 188. Other quotations from the *Vision* are from the pages following.
8. See Frank Kermode's note to iv. i. 148 in the New Arden edition of the play (London, 1962) and his excellent summary discussion on masque-form and *The Tempest*, pp. lxxi-vi, and Joan Rees, *Samuel Daniel* (Liverpool, 1964), p. 93. John C. Meagher discusses the differences between Daniel and Jonson in Ch. 1 of *Method and Meaning in Jonson's Masques*.
9. *Holinshed's Chronicles* (London, 1808), iii, 763.
10. See J. J. Scarisbrick, *Henry VIII* (London, 1968), p. 149, and Neville Williams, *Henry VIII and His Court* (London, 1971), p. 105.
11. A galliard or a volta is suggested by Dorothy Richey in *The Dance in the Drama of the Elizabethan Public Theatre*, unpublished dissertation (Northwestern University, 1951), pp. 69–71; for the vision in iv. ii Dr Richey suggests a pavan (pp. 20–3).
12. 'Of this stage direction I do not believe our author wrote one word' was the irascible comment of Malone, who considered the golden vizards 'tawdry disguises' (*The Plays and Poems of William Shakespeare* (London, 1821), xix, 450). W. J. Lawrence, pursuing his belief that all the ceremonial stage directions in the play were non-authorial, suggests that those for the vision were written by the arranger of the dance. See *Times Literary Supplement*, 18 Dec. 1930, and a rejoinder by Peter Alexander in the issue for 1 Jan. 1931. There is no clear evidence to support the views of either Malone or Lawrence.
13. See also G. Whitney, *A Choice of Emblemes* (1586; repr., 1969), p. 118, and relevant entries in George Ferguson, *Signs and Symbols in Christian Art* (New York, 1961), and Ad de Vries, *Dictionary of Symbols and Imagery* (Amsterdam, 1974). In *The Terrors of the Night* (1594) Thomas Nashe describes with characteristic energy and humour the vision of a dying gentleman whose room is invaded by a variety of dancing apparitions. Unlike Queen Katherine's spirits, these are evil, and they vanish when the gentleman drinks 'a most precious extract quintessence' (sig. G4).
14. Tyrone Guthrie's Stratford production of 1949 dispensed with the spirits and their dancing so far as the audience was concerned, but cunningly included the vision nonetheless; as Muriel St Clare Byrne reported, Katherine 'dropped asleep, and then, opening her eyes, saw the vision in the vacant air above our heads, playing the whole thing straight to us. It was finely and convincingly done' [*Shakespeare Survey, 3* (1950), 128]. Guthrie also did away with the coronation procession, presenting it mainly through the eyes of the bystanders of iv. i.
15. See Louis B. Wright, 'Vaudeville Dancing and Acrobatics in Elizabethan Plays', *Englische Studien*, 63 (1928), 59–76.
16. Daniel, op. cit., 194; Jonson, op. cit., 191, 315–16.

## CHAPTER 8

1. Dorothy Richey found that of 237 plays from *c.* 1580 to 1630, selected apparently at random, 68, or rather less than a third, call for dancing. (See *Summaries of Doctoral Dissertations*, xix (1952), 169.) On the play within the play

see Arthur Brown, 'The Play within the Play: an Elizabethan Dramatic Device', *Essays and Studies*, n.s. 13 (1960), 36–48, and on the dumb show see Dieter Mehl, *The Elizabethan Dumb Show* (London, 1965), pp. 109–37.

2. *Coriolanus* is exceptional in that 'dance' occurs twice in Act v (iii. 99 and iv. 51) and 'dances' in Act iv (v. 116); each use is metaphorical.

3. These were for a number of masques presented after 1616. See *Ben Jonson*, x, 267, and J. C. Meagher, op. cit., p. 202.

# Bibliography

The items listed have been cited in the Notes section.

Alexander, Peter, 'The Coronation in "King Henry VIII"', *Times Literary Supplement*, 1 January 1931, p. 12.

Altick, Richard, 'Symphonic Imagery in *Richard II*', *PMLA*, lxii (1947), 339–45.

Arbeau, Thoinot [Jehan Tabourot], *Orchésographie* (Lengres, 1589).

——, *Orchésographie*, trans. C. W. Beaumont (London, 1925).

——, *Orchésographie*, trans. Mary Stewart Evans (New York, 1967).

Ascham, Roger, *The Schoolmaster* (1573).

Axton, Marie, 'Robert Dudley and the Inner Temple Revels', *Historical Journal*, xiii (1970), 365–70.

Barber, C. L., *Shakespeare's Festive Comedy* (Princeton, N. J., 1959).

Barton, Anne, ' "As you Like It" and "Twelfth Night": Shakespeare's Sense of an Ending', in *Shakespearian Comedy*, ed. Malcolm Bradbury and David Palmer (London, 1972).

Baskervill, Charles, *The Elizabethan Jig* (Chicago, 1929).

Bentley, G. E., *The Jacobean and Caroline Stage*, 7 vols (Oxford, 1941–68).

Brissenden, Alan, ' "Much Ado About Nothing", ii. i. 86–96: The Case for Balthasar', *Notes and Queries*, n.s. 26, 2 (1979), 116–17.

——, 'Shakespeare and the Morris', *Review of English Studies*, n.s. xxx, 117 (1979), 1–11.

Brooke, Arthur, *The Tragicall History of Romeus and Juliet*, ed. P. A. Daniel (London, 1875).

Brooks, Eric St. John, *Sir Christopher Hatton* (London, 1947).

Brown, Arthur, 'The Play within the Play: an Elizabethan Dramatic Device', *Essays and Studies*, n.s. 13 (1960), 36–48.

Brown, John Russell, *Shakespeare and his Comedies* (London, 1957).

Brydges, Sir E., *The British Bibliographer* (vol. 4 by Sir E. Brydges and Joseph Haslewood), 4 vols (London, 1810–14).

Bullough, Geoffrey, *Narrative and Dramatic Sources of Shakespeare*, 8 vols (London, 1957–75).

Burton, Robert, *The Anatomy of Melancholy*, ed. F. Dell and P. Jordan-Smith (New York, 1938).

Byrne, Muriel St. Clare, 'A Stratford Production: *Henry VIII*', *Shakespeare Survey*, 3 (1950), 120–9.

*Calendar of Patent Rolls, Elizabeth I*, vol. 6 (1572–5) ed. N. Williams (London, 1973).

*Calendar of State Papers, Domestic Series, Elizabeth, 1601–1603*, ed. Mary Anne Everett Green (London, 1870; repr. 1967).

Caroso, Fabritio, *Della Nobiltà di Dame* (Venice, 1600).

Cartari, Vincenzo, *Le Imagini de i Dei de gli Antichi* (Venice, 1571; repr. 1976).

Case, John, *The Praise of Musicke*, 1586.

Castiglione, Baldassare, *The Book of the Courtier*, trans. Sir Thomas Hoby, ed. W. E. Henley (London, 1900).

Chamberlain, John, *Letters*, ed. Norman E. McClure, 2 vols (Philadelphia, 1939).

Chambers, E. K., *The Elizabethan Stage*, 4 vols (Oxford, 1928).

——, *The Medieval Stage*, 2 vols (London, 1925).

——, *William Shakespeare*, 2 vols (Oxford, 1963).

Clemen, Wolfgang, *A Commentary on Shakespeare's 'Richard III'* (London, 1968).

——, *The Development of Shakespeare's Imagery* (London, 1951).

Collier, J. P., *Annals of the Stage* (London, 1831).

Collins, A. S., '*Timon of Athens*: A Reconsideration', *Review of English Studies*, XXII (1946), 96–108.

Comes, N., *Mythologie*, trans. I. de Montlyard (Lyon, 1607).

Cook, David, '*Timon of Athens*', *Shakespeare Survey*, 16 (1963), 83–94.

Coplande, Robert, . . . *the maner of dauncynge of bace dauuces* . . . (1521).

Cunningham, J. P., *Dancing at the Inns of Court* (London, 1965).

Curry, W. C., *Shakespeare's Philosophical Patterns* (Baton Rouge, 1937).

Daniel, Samuel, *Complete Works*, ed. A. B. Grosart, 4 vols (Blackburn, 1885).

Davies, Sir John, *The Poems*, ed. Robert Krueger (Oxford, 1975).

Dee, John, Preface to Henry Billingsley, *Elements of Geometrie* (1570).

Dennis, John, *The Comical Gallant* (London, 1702).

*A Dialogue Betweene Custom and Veritie concerning the Vse and Abuse of Dancing and Minstrelsie* (1581).

Donaldson, Ian, '*All's Well That Ends Well*: Shakespeare's Play of Endings', *Essays in Criticism*, XXVII, 1 (1977), 34–55.

Edwards, Philip, 'Shakespeare's Romances: 1900–1957', *Shakespeare Survey*, II (1958), 1–18.

Elyot, Sir Thomas, *The Book named the Governor*, ed. S. E. Lehmberg (London, 1962).

Erasmus, Desiderius, *The Education of a Christian Prince*, trans. Lester K. Born (New York, 1965).

Ewbank, Inga-Stina, 'These Pretty Devices', in *A Book of Masques*, gen. ed. T. J. B. Spencer (Cambridge, 1966).

Felperin, Howard, *Shakespearean Romance* (Princeton, N.J., 1972).

Ferguson, George, *Signs and Symbols in Christian Art* (New York, 1961).

Fetherston, Christopher, *A Dialogue agaynst light, lewde, and lasciuious daunting* (1582).

Ficino, Marsilio, *Sopra l'Amore o Vero Convito di Platone* (Florence, 1594).

Field, John, *A Godly Exhortation, by occasion of the late iudgement of God, showed at Paris Garden* (1583).

Foakes, R. A., *Shakespeare: From the Dark Comedies to the Last Plays* (London, 1971).

——, 'Voices of Maturity in Shakespeare's Comedies', in *Shakespearian Comedy*, ed. Malcolm Bradbury and David Palmer (London, 1972).

Fowler, Alastair, 'Leontes' Contrition and the Repair of Nature', *Essays and Studies*, n.s. 31 (1978), 36–64.

Froissart, Jean, *The Chronicle of Froissart*, trans. Lord Berners, 6 vols (London, 1901–3).

Gardner, Helen, "As You Like It", in *More Talking About Shakespeare*, ed. John Garrett (London, 1959).

Gombosi, Otto, 'Some Musical Aspects of the English Court Masque', *Journal of the American Musicological Society*, I, 3 (1948), 3–19.

Gosson, Stephen, *The School of Abuse*, ed. J. P. Collier (London, 1841; Shakespeare Society).

Granville-Barker, H., *Prefaces to Shakespeare*, 5 vols (London, 1927–48).

Green, William, *Shakespeare's 'Merry Wives of Windsor'* (Princeton, N.J., 1962).

Harrison, G. B., *A Jacobean Journal* (London, 1946).

Heninger, S. K. Jnr, *Touches of Sweet Harmony* (San Marino, 1974).

Holinshed, Raphael, *Chronicles of England, Scotland and Ireland*, 6 vols (London, 1807–8).

Hotson, Leslie, *The First Night of 'Twelfth Night'* (London, 1961).

——, *Shakespeare versus Shallow* (London, 1931).

Jeffreys, M. D. W., 'The Weird Sisters in *Macbeth*', *English Studies in Africa*, I (1958), 43–54, 229–35.

Jonson, Ben, *Ben Jonson*, ed. C. H. Herford and P. and E. Simpson, 11 vols (Oxford, 1925–52).

Kirk, Robert, *Secret Commonwealth* (Edinburgh, 1815).

Knight, G. Wilson, *The Crown of Life* (London, 1961).

*Larousse Encyclopedia of Mythology*, trans. R. Aldington and D. Ames (London, 1960).

Lawrence, W. J., 'The Stage Directions in "King Henry VIII"', *Times Literary Supplement*, 18 December 1930, p. 1085.

Legh, Gerard, *Accedens of Armory* (1562).

Lodge, Edmund, *Illustrations of British History*, 3 vols (London, 1938; repr. 1969).

Long, John H., *Shakespeare's Use of Music*, 2 vols (Gainesville, Florida, 1955–61).

Lowe, Barbara, 'Early Records of the Morris in England', *Journal of the English Folk Dance and Song Society*, VIII, 2 (1957), 61–82.

Lucian, *The Dance*, trans. A. M. Harmon (London, 1934; Loeb Classical Library).

McGowan, Margaret, *L'Art du ballet de cour* . . . (Paris, 1963).

Mahood, M., *Shakespeare's Wordplay* (London, 1957).

de Maisse, A. H., *Journal*, trans. G. B. Harrison and R. A. Jones (London, 1931).

Major, John M., 'The Moralization of the Dance in Elyot's *Governor*', *Studies in the Renaissance*, V (1958), 27–36.

Manuscripts, Bodleian Library, Oxford. Douce 208; Rawl. Poet., 108; Rawl., d. 864.

Marston, John, *The Insatiate Countesse* (1613).

Meagher, John C., *Method and Meaning in Jonson's Masques* (Notre Dame, Indiana, 1966).

Mehl, Dieter, *The Elizabethan Dumb Show* (London, 1965).

de Mille, Agnes, *The Book of the Dance* (London, 1963).

Moore, O. H., *The Legend of Romeo and Juliet* (Columbus, 1950).

Morley, Thomas, *A Plaine and Easie Introduction to Practicall Musicke* (1597).

Mulcaster, Richard, *Positions*, ed. R. H. Quick (London, 1888).

Nashe, Thomas, *The Terrors of the Night* (1594).

Negri, Cesare, *Nuove Inventione di Balli* (Milan, 1604).

Nichols, John, *The Progresses . . . of Queen Elizabeth*, 2 vols (London, 1788).

Nicoll, Allardyce, 'Shakespeare and the Court Masque', *Shakespeare Jahrbuch*, XCIV (1958), 51–62.

Northbrooke, John, *A Treatise wherein Dicing, Dauncing, Vaine playes or Enterluds . . . are reproued*, ed. J. P. Collier (London, 1843; Shakes. Soc.).

*Old Meg of Hereford-Shire for a Mayd Marian: And Hereford Towne for a Morris-daunce* (1609).

Orgel, Stephen, *The Jonsonian Masque* (Cambridge, Mass., 1965).

Paul, H. N., *The Royal Play of Macbeth* (New York, 1950).

Playford, John, *The English Dancing Master* (1652).

Plutarch, *Shakespeare's Plutarch*, ed. T. J. B. Spencer (Harmondsworth, 1964).

da Porto, Luigi, *Hystoria Nouellamente . . .* (Venice, n.d.).

Prest, W. R., *The Inns of Court* (London, 1972).

Prynne, William, *Histriomastix* (1633).

Rabelais, François, *The Heroic Deeds of Gargantua and Pantagruel* (London, 1951).

Rainoldes, D. [John], *Ouerthrow of Stage-Plays* (1629).

Rand, E. K., *Founders of the Middle Ages* (New York, 1957).

Rees, Joan, *Samuel Daniel* (Liverpool, 1964).

Reyher, Paul, *Les Masques Anglais* (Paris, 1909; repr. 1964).

Rich, Barnaby, *Rich's Farewell to Military Profession*, ed. Thomas M. Cranfell (Austin, 1959).

Richey, Dorothy, 'The Dance in the Drama of the Elizabethan Public Theatre: A Production Problem', *Summaries of Doctoral Dissertations*, Northwestern University, Evanston, Illinois, XIX (1952), 169–74.

——, 'The Dance in the Drama of the Elizabethan Public Theatre: A Production Problem', unpublished dissertation, Northwestern University, Evanston, Illinois (1951).

Rossiter, A. P., *Angel with Horns* (London, 1961).

Rye, W. B., *England as Seen by Foreigners* (London, 1865).

Sabol, Andrew, *Songs and Dances for the Stuart Masque* (Providence, 1959).

——, *Four Hundred Songs and Dances from the Stuart Masque* (Providence, 1978).

Scarisbrick, J. J., *Henry VIII* (London, 1968).

Seneca, *De Beneficiis*, trans. Arthur Golding (1578).

Shakespeare, William, *The Complete Works*, ed. Peter Alexander (London, 1951).

——, *The Plays*, ed. Samuel Johnson and George Steevens, 10 vols (London, 1778).

——, *The Plays and Poems*, ed. James Boswell, 21 vols (London, 1821).

——, *Antony and Cleopatra*, ed. M. R. Ridley (London, 1964; New Arden edn).

——, *Cymbeline*, ed. J. C. Maxwell (Cambridge, 1960; New Shakespeare edn).

——, *Henry V*, ed. J. H. Walter (London, 1954; New Arden edn).

——, *The Second Part of Henry VI*, ed. Andrew S. Cairncross (London, 1962; New Arden edn).

——, *Henry VIII*, ed. A. R. Humphreys (Harmondsworth, 1968; New Penguin edn).

——, *Love's Labour's Lost*, ed. R. David (London, 1951; New Arden edn).

——, *Macbeth*, ed. Kenneth Muir (London, 1962; New Arden edn).

——, *The Merry Wives of Windsor*, ed. H. C. Hart (London, 1904; Arden edn).

——, *The Merry Wives of Windsor*, ed. G. R. Hibbard (Harmondsworth, 1973; New Penguin edn).

——, *The Merry Wives of Windsor*, ed. H. J. Oliver (London, 1971; New Arden edn).

——, *A Midsummer Night's Dream*, ed. Stanley Wells (Harmondsworth, 1968; New Penguin edn).

——, *Much adoe about Nothing* (1600).

——, *Pericles*, ed. Philip Edwards (Harmondsworth, 1973; New Penguin edn).

——, *Pericles*, ed. F. D. Hoeniger (London, 1963; New Arden edn).

——, *Richard II*, ed. Matthew Black (Philadelphia, 1955; New Variorum edn).

——, *Richard II*, ed. P. Ure (London, 1961; New Arden edn).

——, *Richard III*, ed. John Dover Wilson (Cambridge, 1966; New Cambridge edn).

——, *The Tempest*, ed. H. H. Furness (Philadelphia, 1892; Variorum edn).

——, *The Tempest*, ed. Frank Kermode (London, 1962; New Arden edn).

——, *Timon of Athens*, ed. J. C. Maxwell (Cambridge, 1957; New Shakespeare edn).

——, *Twelfth Night*, ed. T. W. Craik (London, 1975; New Arden edn).

——, *Twelfth Night*, ed. H. H. Furness (Philadelphia, 1901; repr. 1964; Variorum edn).

——, *The Winter's Tale*, ed. H. H. Furness (Philadelphia, 1898; repr. 1964; Variorum edn).

——, *The Winter's Tale*, ed. J. H. P. Pafford (London, 1967; New Arden edn).

Sharp, Cecil J. and MacIlwaine, Herbert C., *The Morris Book*, 2nd edn, 3 vols (London, 1912–24).

Sidney, Sir Philip, *The Countesse of Pembrokes Arcadia* (1590).

Sinclair, George, *Satan's Invisible World Discovered* (Edinburgh, 1685).

Sisson, C. J., *New Readings in Shakespeare*, 2 vols (Cambridge, 1956).

Smith, Hallett, *Shakespeare's Romances* (San Marino, 1972).

Sorell, Walter, 'Shakespeare and the Dance', *Shakespeare Quarterly*, VIII (1957), 367–84.

Spencer, T. J. B. (gen. ed.), *A Book of Masques in honour of Allardyce Nicoll* (London, 1966).

Spurgeon, C. F. E., *Shakespeare's Imagery* (Cambridge, 1935).

Steadman, John M., 'Falstaff as Actaeon: A Dramatic Emblem', *Shakespeare Quarterly*, XIV (1963), 231–44.

Sternfeld, F. W., *Music in Shakespearian Tragedy* (Oxford, 1962).

Strong, Roy, *Splendour at Court* (London, 1973).

Strong, Roy and Orgel, Stephen, *Inigo Jones*, 2 vols (London, 1973).

Strong, Roy, 'Inigo Jones and the Revival of Chivalry', *Apollo*, LXXXVI (1967), 102–7.

Stubbes, Philip, *The Anatomy of Abuses*, ed. F. S. Furnivall (London, 1877–82; New Shakespeare Society).

Tanner, J. R., *Constitutional Documents of the Reign of James I* (Cambridge, 1961).

Tilley, M. P., *A Dictionary of the Proverbs of England in the 16th and 17th Centuries* (Ann Arbor, 1950).

Topsell, Edward, *The Historie of Foure Footed Beastes* (1607).

Vives, Juan Luis, *Linguae Latinae Exercitatio*, trans. Forster Watson (London, 1970).

de Vries, Ad, *Dictionary of Symbols and Imagery* (Amsterdam, 1974).

Vyvyan, J., *Shakespeare and Platonic Beauty* (London, 1961).

Ward, John M., 'The maner of dauncyng', *Early Music*, 4 (1976), 127–42.

Wells, Stanley, *Shakespeare* (Oxford, 1973; Select Bibliographical Guides).

Welsford, Enid, *The Court Masque* (Cambridge, 1927).

Whitney, George, *A Choice of Emblemes* (1586, repr. 1969).

Wilkins, George, *The Painfull Aduentures of Pericles Prince of Tyre*, ed. Kenneth Muir (Liverpool, 1967).

Wilson, John Dover, *Shakespeare's Happy Comedies* (London, 1962).

Williams, Neville, *Henry VIII and His Court* (London, 1971).

Wind, Edgar, *Pagan Mysteries in the Renaissance* (London, 1958).

Wood, Melusine, *Some Historical Dances* (London, 1952).

Wright, Louis B., 'Vaudeville Dancing and Acrobatics in Elizabethan Plays', *Englische Studien*, 63 (1928), 59–76.

Yates, Frances A., 'Elizabethan Chivalry: The Romance of the Accession Day Tilts', *Journal of the Warburg and Courtauld Institutes*, XX, 1 (1957), 4–25.

——, *Shakespeare's Last Plays* (London, 1975).

——, *The Valois Tapestries* (London, 1975).

## DANCES FOR THE PLAYS

The following contemporary dances are suggested as a basis for choreographers and directors:

| | | |
|---|---|---|
| *All's Well That Ends Well**  | II. iii. 37 | coranto (a few steps) |
| *Antony and Cleopatra* | II. vii. 120 | drunken steps, based on a brawl |
| *As You Like It* | V. iv. 192 | pavan (the measures) |
| *Cymbeline** | V. iv. 29 | pavan |
| *Henry VIII* | I. iv. 76 | pavan and galliard, coranto or volta |
| | IV. ii. 82 | pavan |
| *Love's Labour's Lost** | V. ii. 916 | hay |
| *Macbeth* | I. iii. 32 | carole |
| | †IV. i. 133 | grotesque round dance |

\* Dancing is probable rather than certain.
† Not Shakespearian.

| | | |
|---|---|---|
| *The Merry Wives of Windsor* | v. v. 90 | carole |
| *A Midsummer Night's Dream* | ii. ii. 8 | carole |
| | iv. i. 83 | pavan, almain |
| | v. i. 350 | bergomask |
| | v. i. 389 | carole |
| *Much Ado About Nothing* | ii. i. 72 | pavan |
| | ii. i. 135 | galliard, volta or coranto |
| | v. iv. 124 | galliard, volta or coranto |
| *Pericles* | ii. iii. 98 | sword dance (matachins) |
| | ii. iii. 107 | pavan |
| *Romeo and Juliet* | i. v. 24 | pavan |
| *The Tempest* | iv. i. 138 | hay, brawl |
| *Timon of Athens* | i. ii. 126 | pavan; galliard, coranto |
| *The Two Noble Kinsmen* | †ii. v. 135 | coranto, galliard or lively brawl |
| *The Winter's Tale* | iv. iv. 165 | brawl, hay |
| | 336 | energetic, grotesque dancing |

# Index